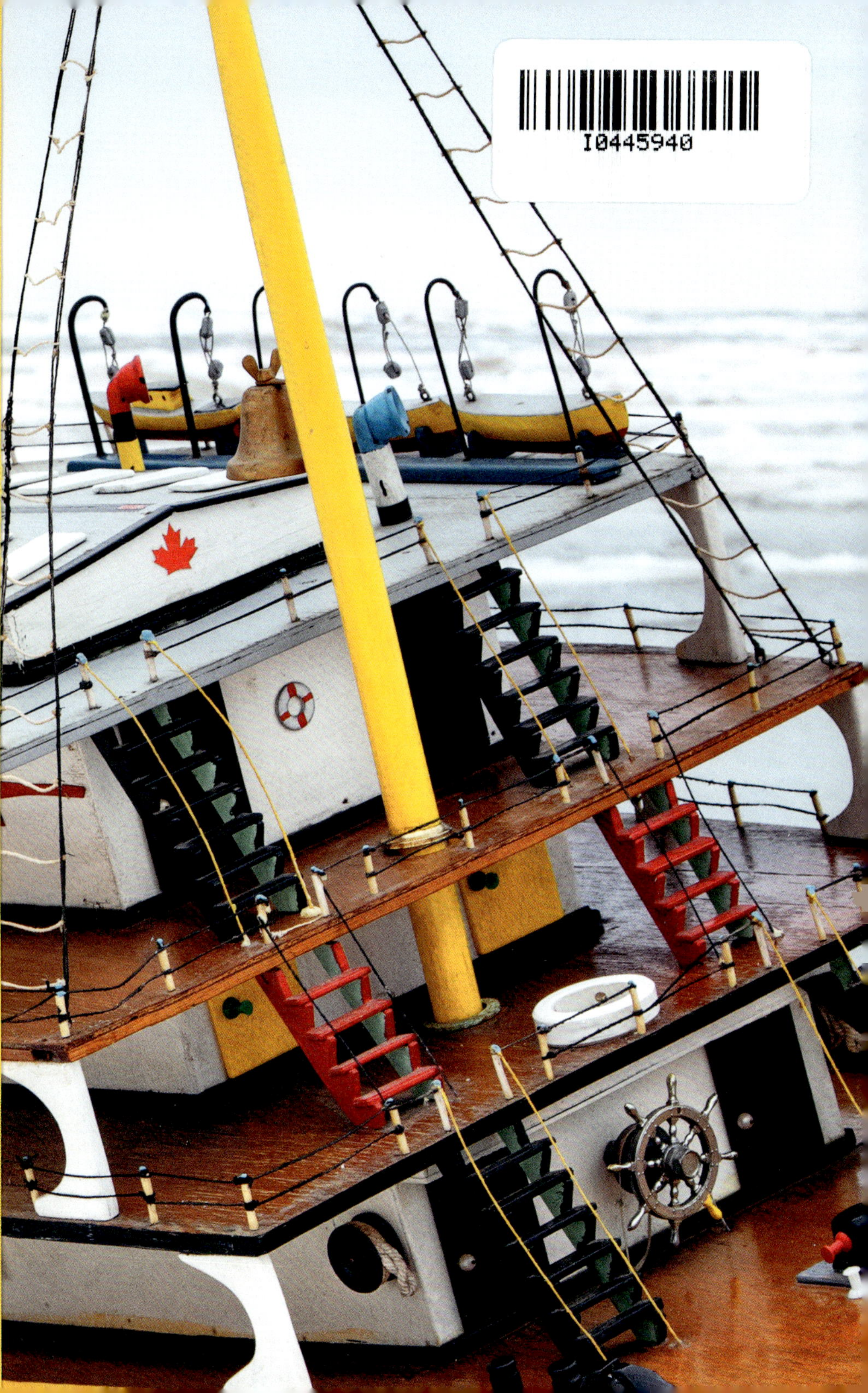

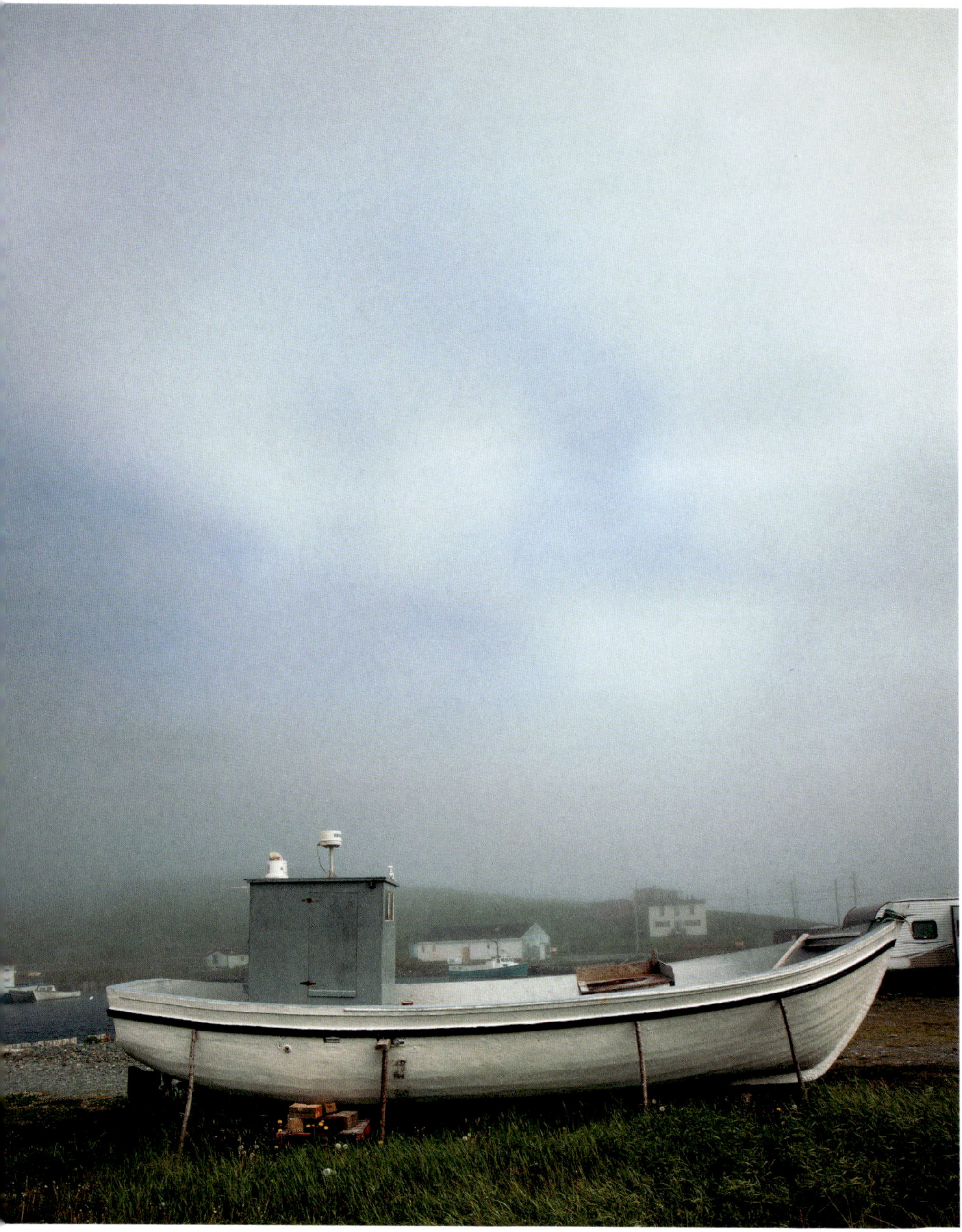

TRAP SKIFF

Ferryland, Newfoundland and Labrador

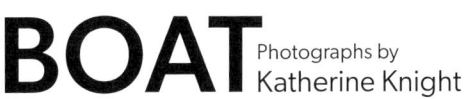

OUT OF THE MUSEUM INTO THE WILD

KATHERINE KNIGHT
Photographer
Filmmaker

Caribou Harbour,
Nova Scotia

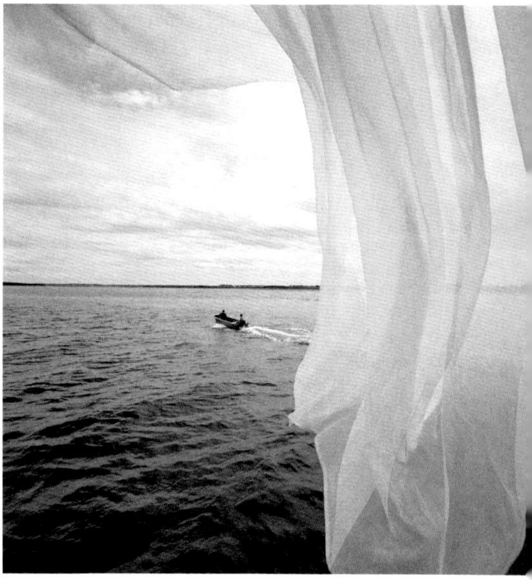

Murray Islands, Prince Edward Island, 1999

BOAT connects handmade models to stories and geographies: memory makers linking Atlantic people and places. Crafted by fishermen in their leisure time or fabricated to plan and commemorate ships—new, old, and remembered—models are the material residue of historical patterns of leisure and labour. With urbanization and economic changes in fishing and shipbuilding, models have faded from view, and the crafts associated with their making are being lost. Distinctive public and private collections exist, but the will to expand them appears diminished.

In 2009, my friend and mentor Colette Urban gifted me a model schooner. Colette was a "come from away" who declared herself home in western Newfoundland after a career living and working elsewhere. Her saltbox home was full of local objects mixed with her own artworks, proof of an intense and celebrated creative life. Colette believed that artifacts and people live in reciprocity. Take this model boat, she said, and then gave me another. As Colette anticipated, *BOAT* worked itself into my imagination and, in time, back into this world.

In 2016, Shelley and Leonard Bigney, fishers from River John, Nova Scotia, built a sled for my largest model and hauled it to Dragline Beach so I could photograph the boat against frozen land and sea. At first glance, the image fits scenic expectations. On closer study, rough-and-ready details—a repurposed thumbtack, a flag sticker or thread spool—reveal the boat's scale and at-hand materials.

This book gathers my purpose-made model boat photographs, interviews, and essays, along with earlier black-and-white photographs from my archive of analog images. Like the models themselves, *BOAT* lays anchor in its maritime home, reanimating the experiences, imaginings, and remembrances both of creators and of those that love this craft.

PUNT

Clayton Dominey, Burgeo, Newfoundland and Labrador

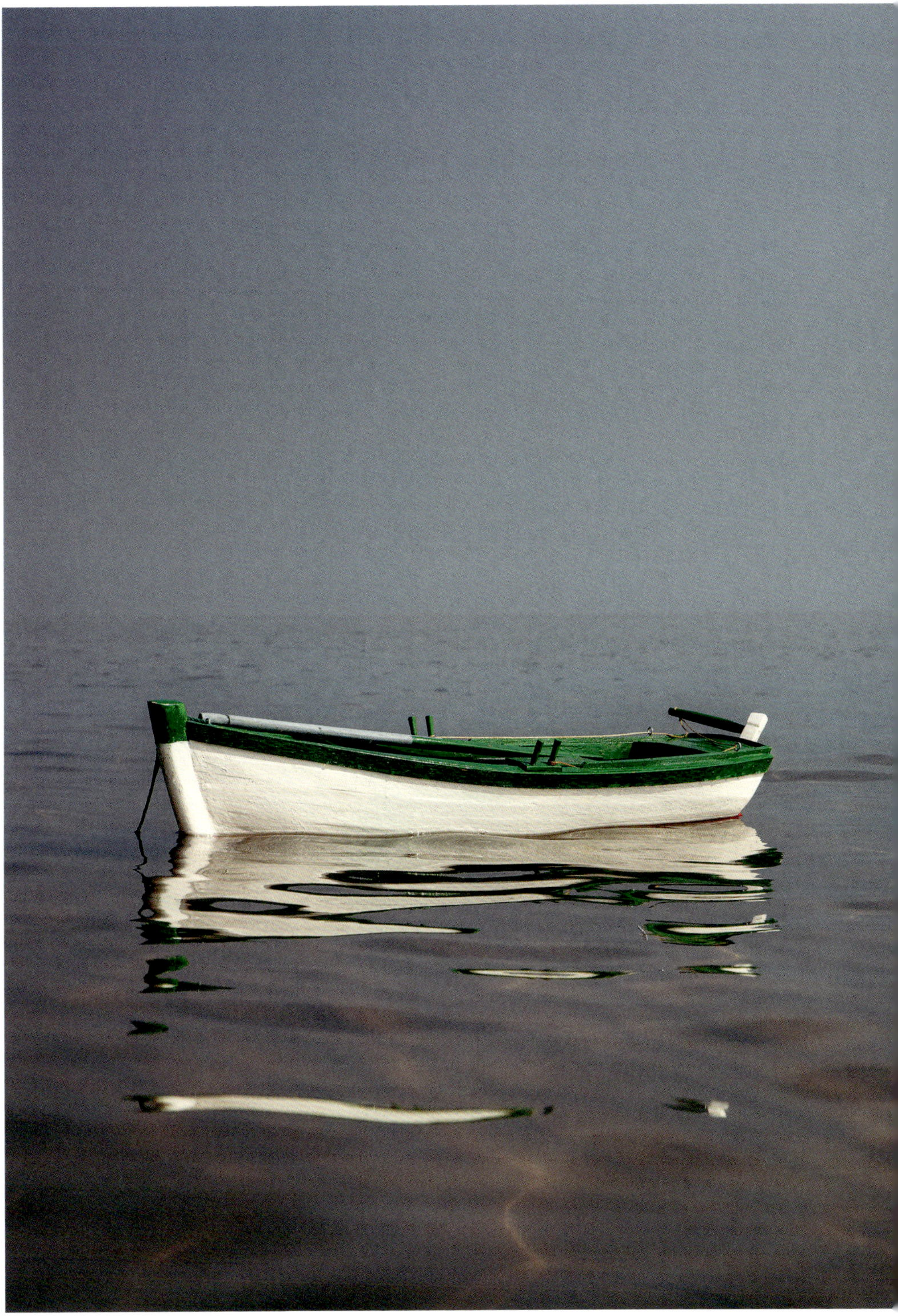

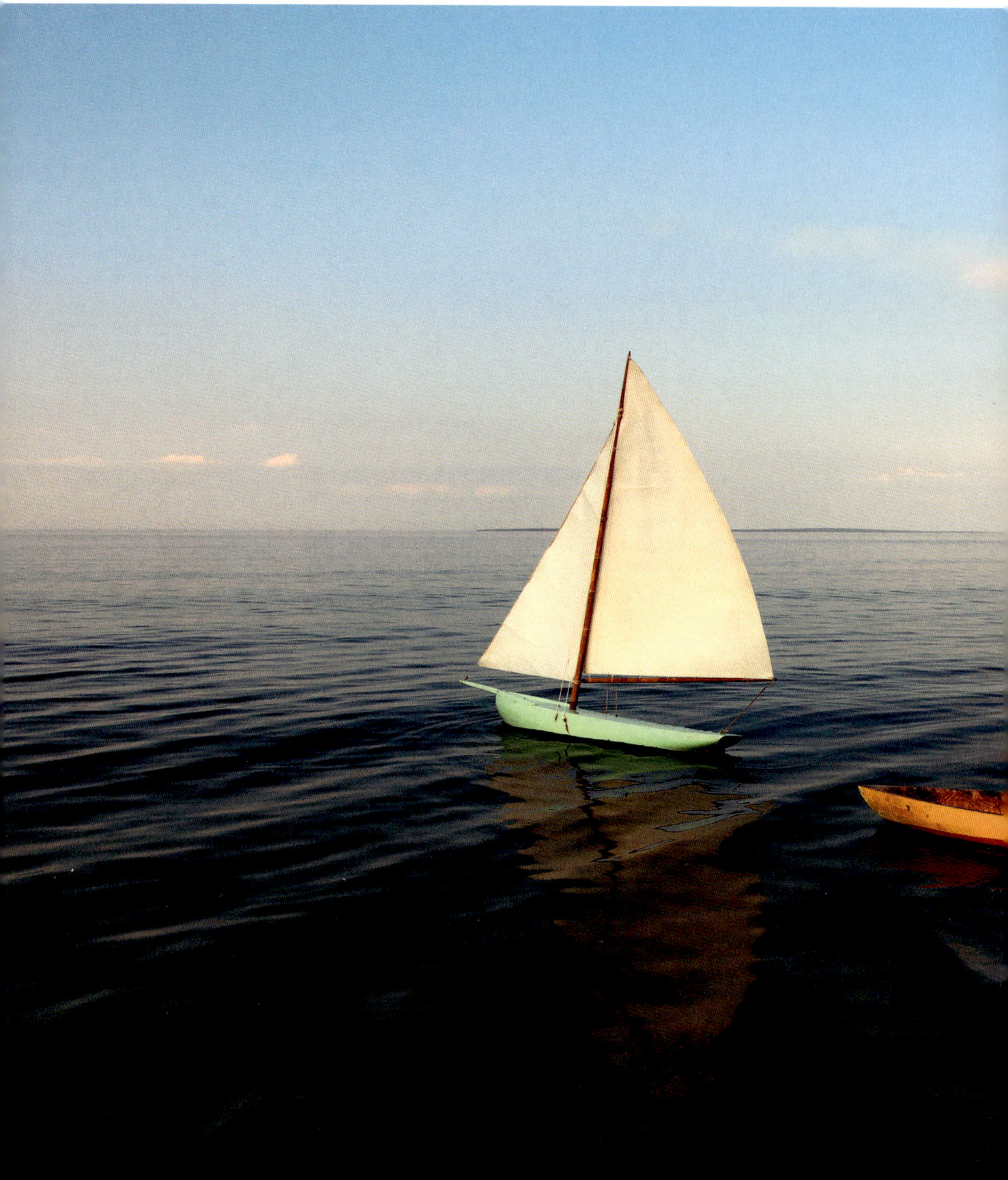

SLOOP & HULL

William Francis Durant, Two Islands, Nova Scotia

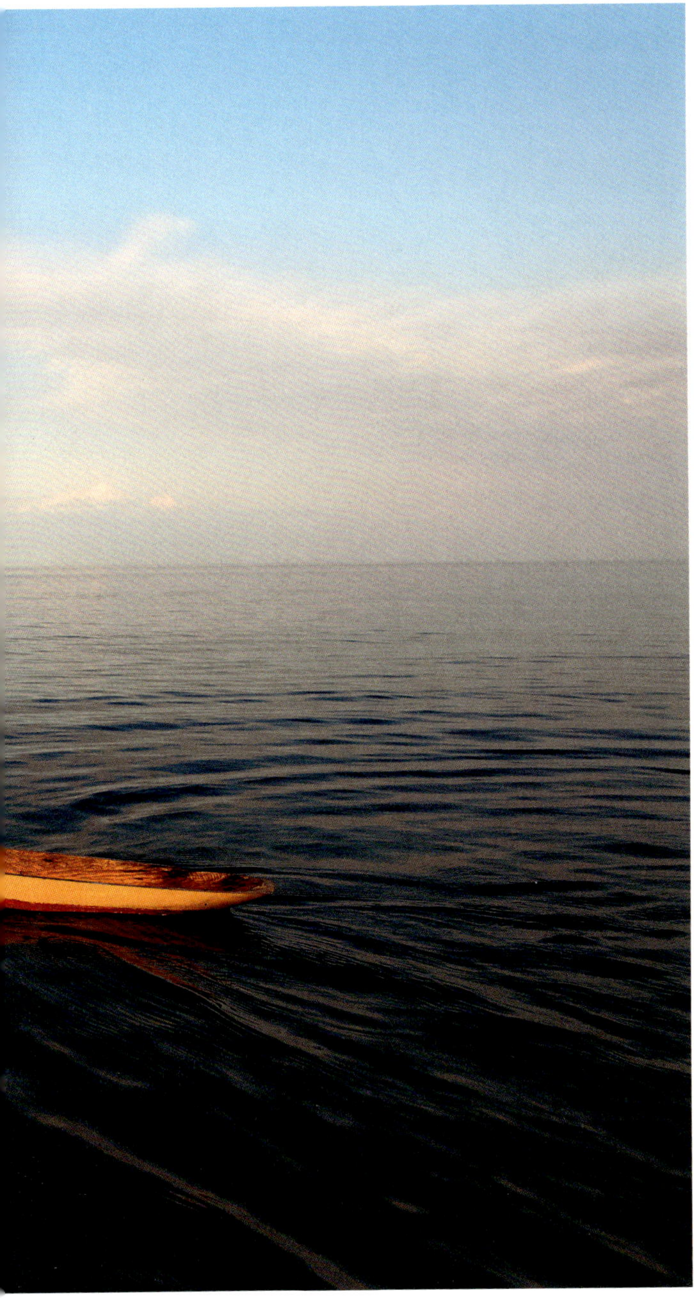

PUNT

Maker unknown, Newfoundland and Labrador

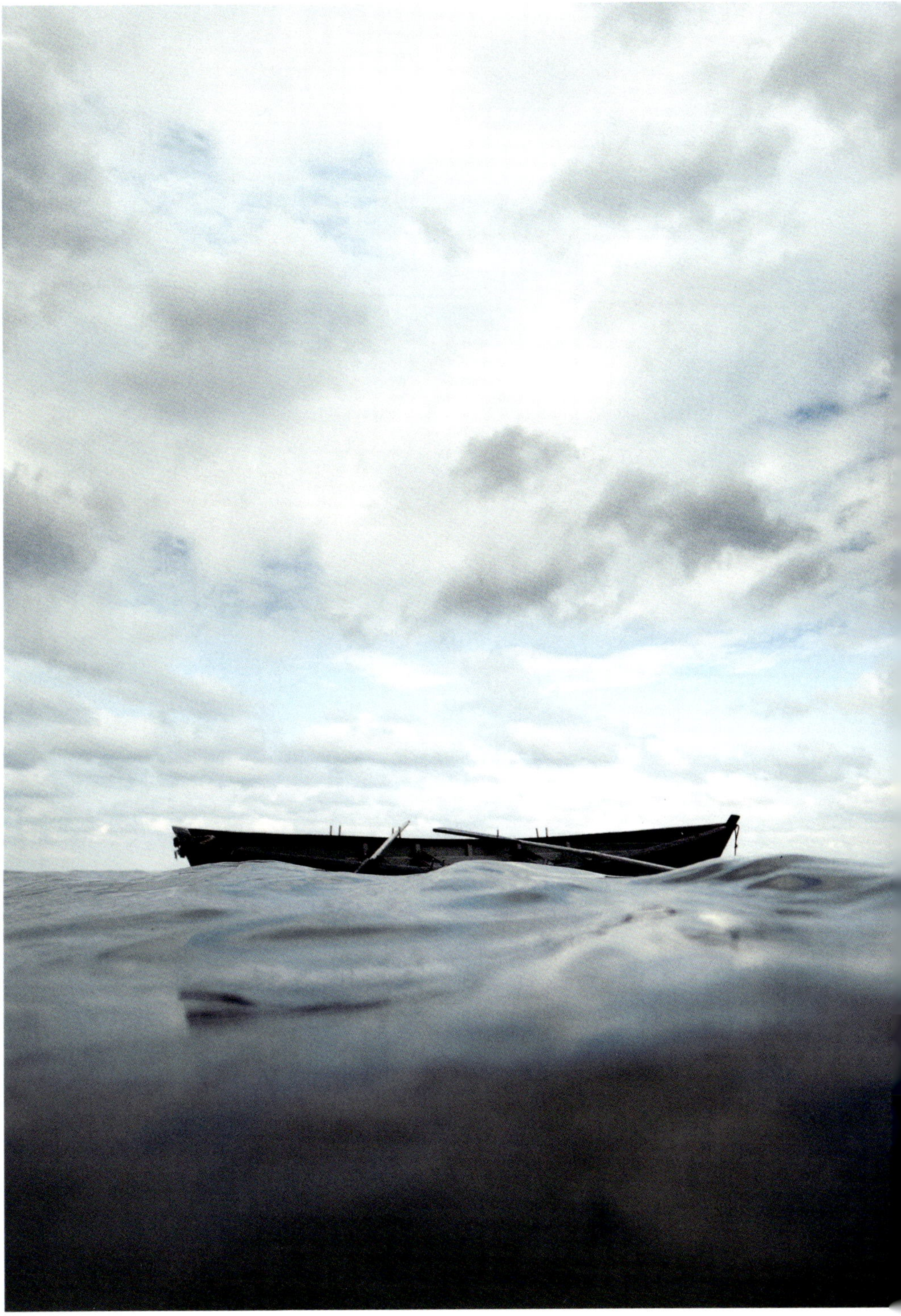

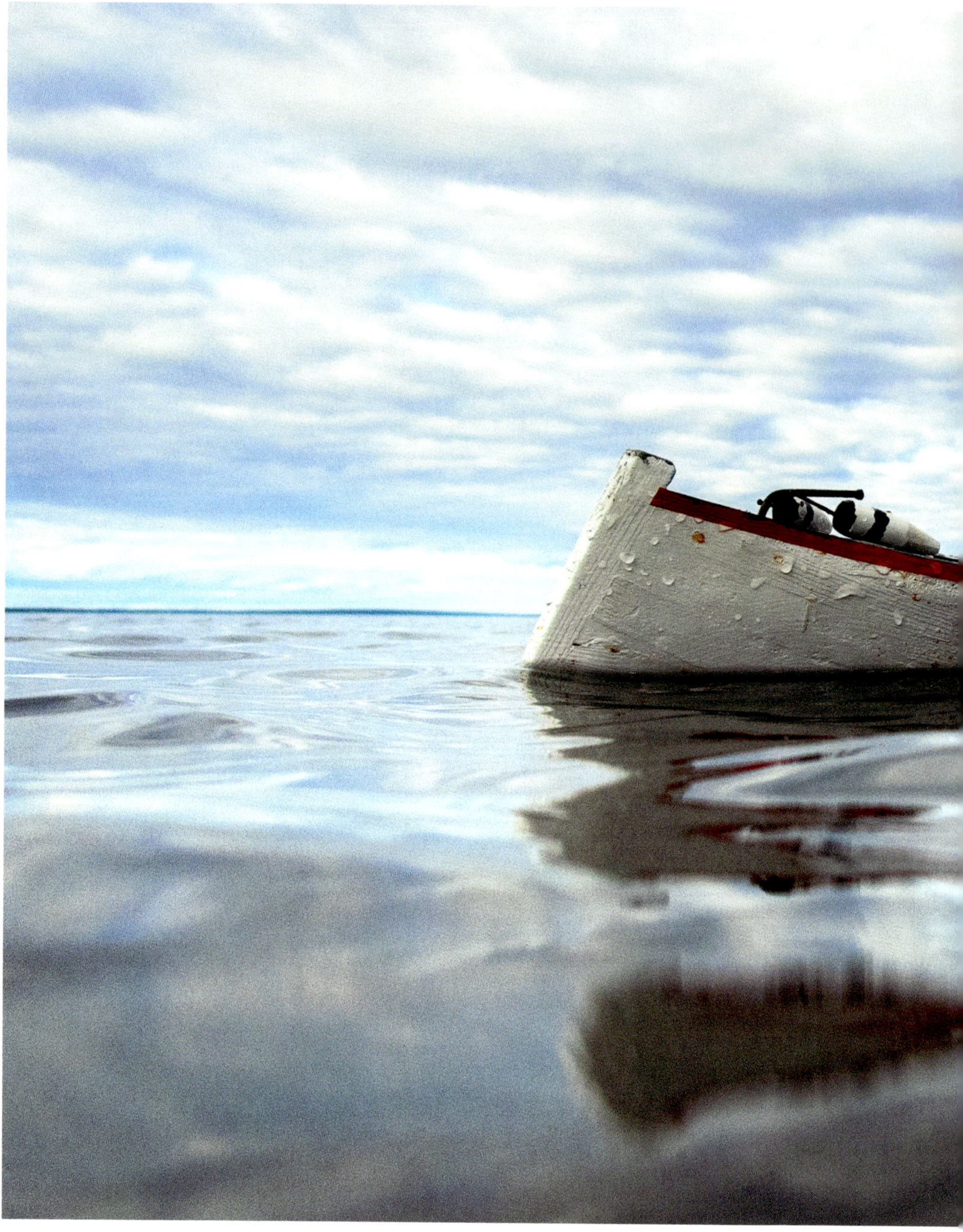

DOUBLE ENDER

Wheaton Gosbee, Abney, Prince Edward Island

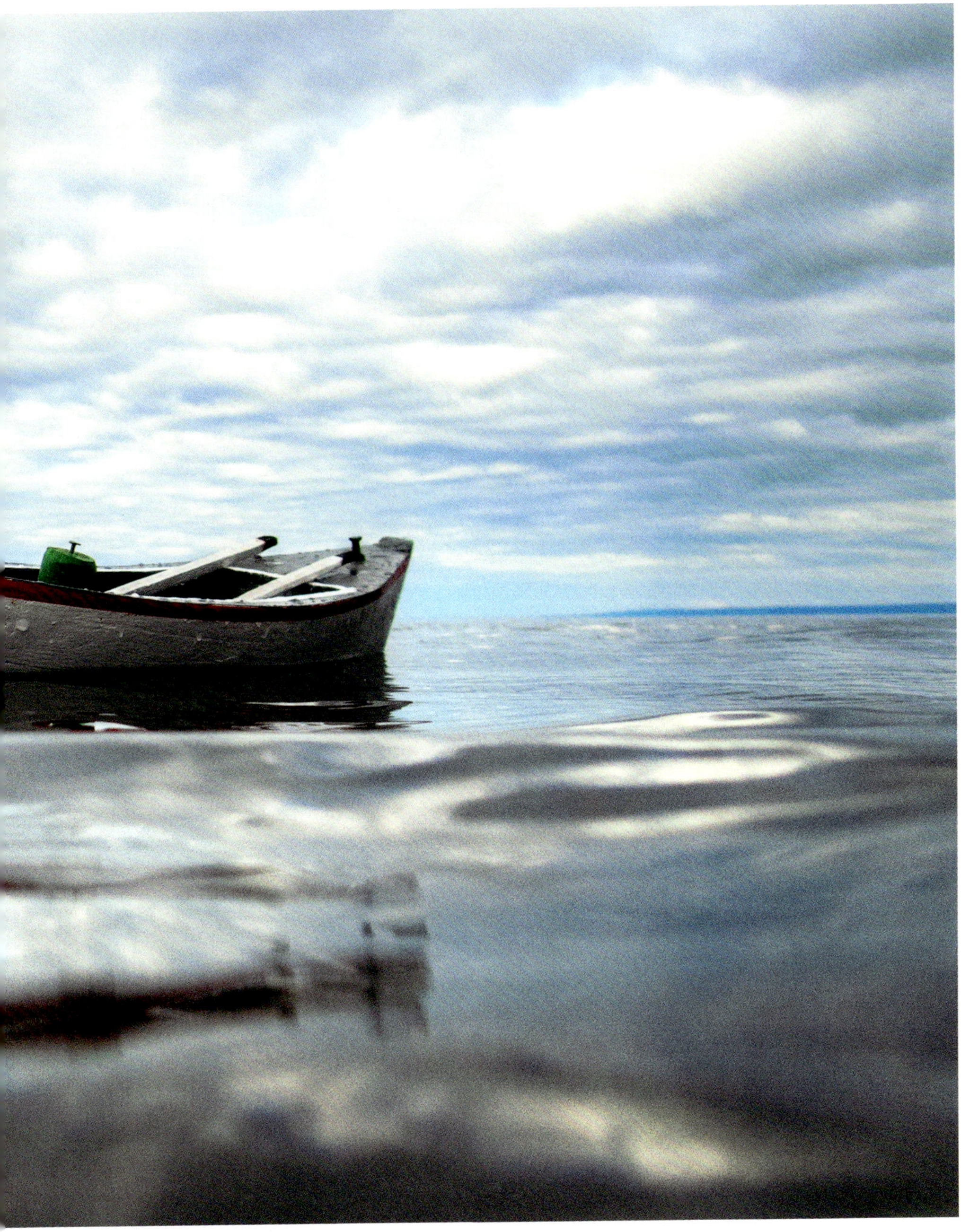

LISTEN FOR WHAT SWIMS

SUE GOYETTE
Poet
Educator

Kjipuktuk,
Halifax,
Nova Scotia

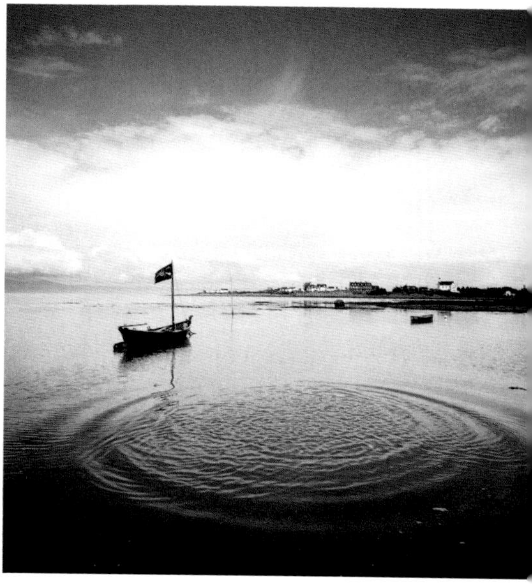

Saint-Jean-Port-Joli, Quebec, 2002

its workday clock. I'm interested in the kind of devotion I mentioned above especially now for how it invites us to move beyond that clock to participate in low-stake making in which hours are spent meaningfully. Doesn't it feel crucial to be doing the kinds of things where our hearts are not only being considered but actively involved? In the way these makers are transforming the memory of a lived experience into something that represents what keeps that memory flared and remembered? This is mapmaking of the highest order. A version of *you are here* that emerges from a solid and embodied *you were there*. An archive of sorts that we'll need for reference in this turbo-changing world.

Before we consider the boats, let's give "model" some space. Repetition is one of the poetic strategies I often use to organize the logic and ecosystem of ideas and images my work is manifesting. It is the juncture between Phillips's transcribing and transformation and a site that shimmers with potential. I align the function of repetition/replication with astrologer Chani Nicholas's *we repeat who we are*[3] in the company of Gertrude Stein's understanding of repetition as being more a genus of insistence than reiteration.[4] When these ideas are given some room to commingle and collaborate, they can add a delectable complexity to the ways repetition and replication work. We repeat and replicate experiences that matter to us to honour their importance as well as to honour who we were in those experiences. A model can be considered both an object (a boat) and a site that holds a recharge of our best selves in the company of the wild expanse of water, land, and sky that holds the memory intact. In this way, the transformative aspect of making is activated as reciprocal. The memory has enriched and transformed the maker's experience into an object *and* the maker has been transformed by the experience of making this lasting memorialization. Working in this register can't help but transform its maker brighter

I'm interested in the species of devotion that calls us to make things. Whatever it is that gets our attention and keeps it. The things we make not for money and not necessarily for the outcome but more for the quality of time we inhabit when possessed by and pursuing that frisson of passion that's hanging onto something just beyond legible. The sacred allure of the unsayable, the yet unnamed that is the sap of our humanity for how it recharges and pollinates us. And the thing we end up making, like all things, holds our fallibility, our coming-close-but-not-quite-getting-it, which is its glory. Not the miss but our attempt, the reach, the risk that making something from nothing takes. Which is one of the finest reasons we try again. To get closer to how vital we feel when we've abandoned getting it perfect and instead revel in the process of being creative. I'm tempted to name that elemental creative verve here and know better. Sheila Heti describes it as the "essential thing, the spark that says *more than here*" in its results.[1] Poet Carl Phillips says poetry is not interested in transcribing experience but rather in transforming it somehow.[2] A seemingly straightforward formula that makes its own great demands on its maker. And responding to the demands of an emerging, manifesting new thing as it becomes itself, incrementally, is how, over time, we establish a creative practice. And that practice becomes another way we breathe.

Bringing these model boats together, after carrying them for as long as it took for them to arrive here, is no small feat. The waters of this singular time are turbulent in a way that is epic and new to us. We are not only enduring a planet in deep crisis but are in the middle of a reckoning with the impact and violence of capitalism, colonialism, and patriarchal, white-bodied supremacy. It is no wonder that our bodies are amped by uppercase fear and anxiety and that we're manifesting an ultra-competent dissonance that is zombie-like and weirdly loyal to the same old and

and closer to who and how they most want to be. Here's when we attend and move into our world keener and more alert, game and ready for anything, which is contagious and can evoke exuberant and lively engagement. Art making is how we recharge and upgrade. How we nourish our imaginative selves, which ensures we are in good enough shape to then imagine better ways of being in the yet-to-come rather than anticipating the worst.

Of course, the big transformation at the heart of this, put simply, is how boats have moved from vessel, water, sky, and shore to models and now to book. And how this book is a boat that will be pulled ashore by many hands.

The inimitable dancer/choreographer Pina Bausch said, "When you create a new work, the point of departure must be contemporary life."[5] What is it about these model boats arriving now when things are as dire as they are? Proof, perhaps, that anything made with love holds something fierce and true about ourselves that we cannot afford to lose right now. How this kind of making in an earlier time may have been considered a hobby or craft but is now an act of resistance. A slowing of time. A blurring of past, present, and future. Each boat then may be an invitation to put down our devices to consider our hands and what we could potentially make. And how, in the making, we remember ourselves and the groove of being okay. And how that groove is deeply attending to what's at hand and what can potentially be coming: on open water, listening for what swims.

1. Sheila Heti, *Pure Colour* (Vintage Canada, 2022), 16.

2. Carl Phillips, "For Carl Phillips, Poetry Is Experience Transformed—Not Transcribed," interview, NPR, August 29, 2015, www.npr.org/2015/08/29/435492413/for-carl-phillips-poetry-is-experience-transformed-not-transcribed.

3. Chani Nicholas, "May 2020 Horoscopes & Cosmic Playlists," May 2020, www.chani.com/blogs/may-2020-horoscopes-cosmic-playlists.

4. "Miss Stein States There Is No Such Thing as Repetition," *Ann Arbor News*, December 15, 1934; see aadl.org/aa_news_19341215_p1-miss_stein_states.

5. Royd Climenhaga, *Pina Bausch* (Routledge, 2009), 50.

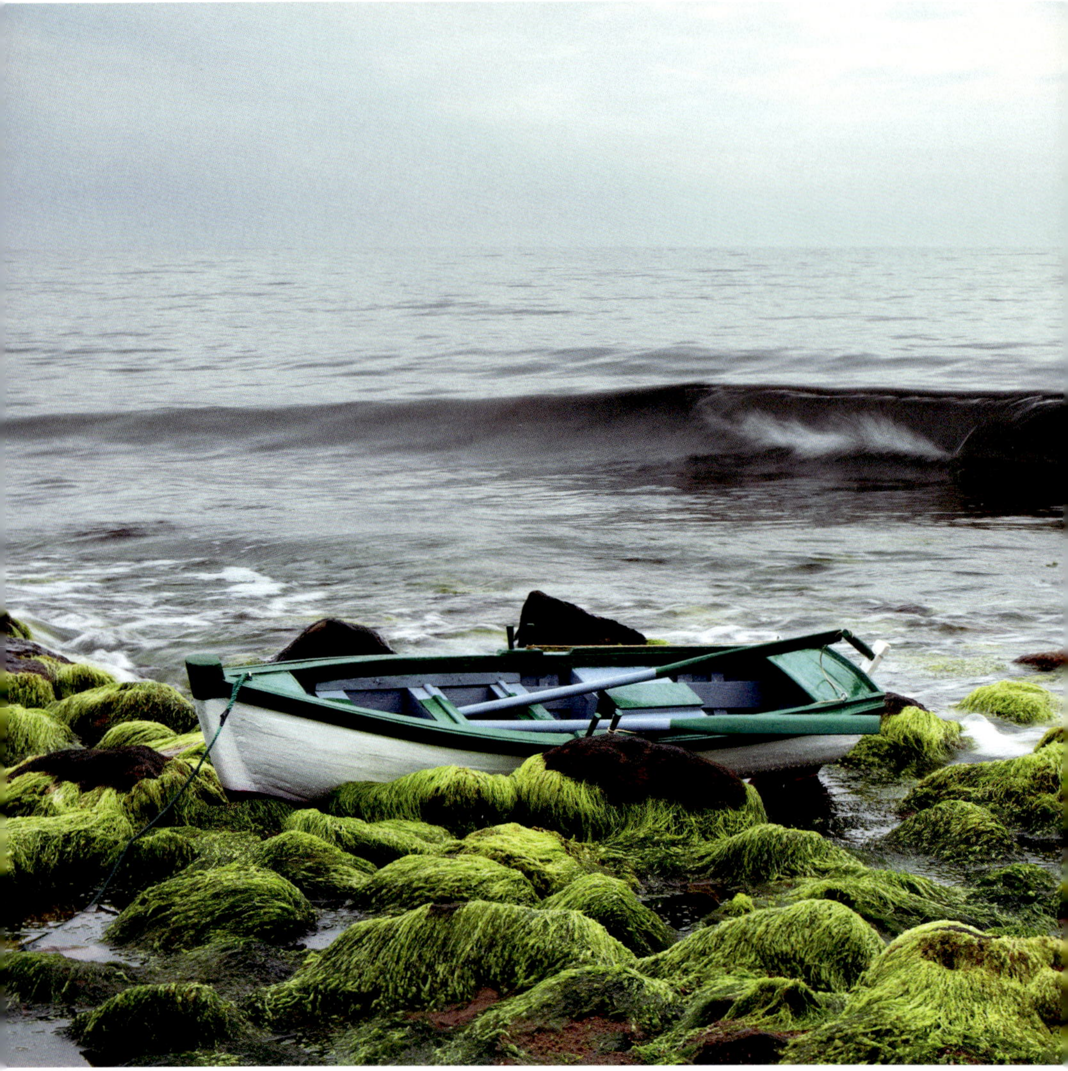

PUNT

Clayton Dominey, Burgeo, Newfoundland and Labrador

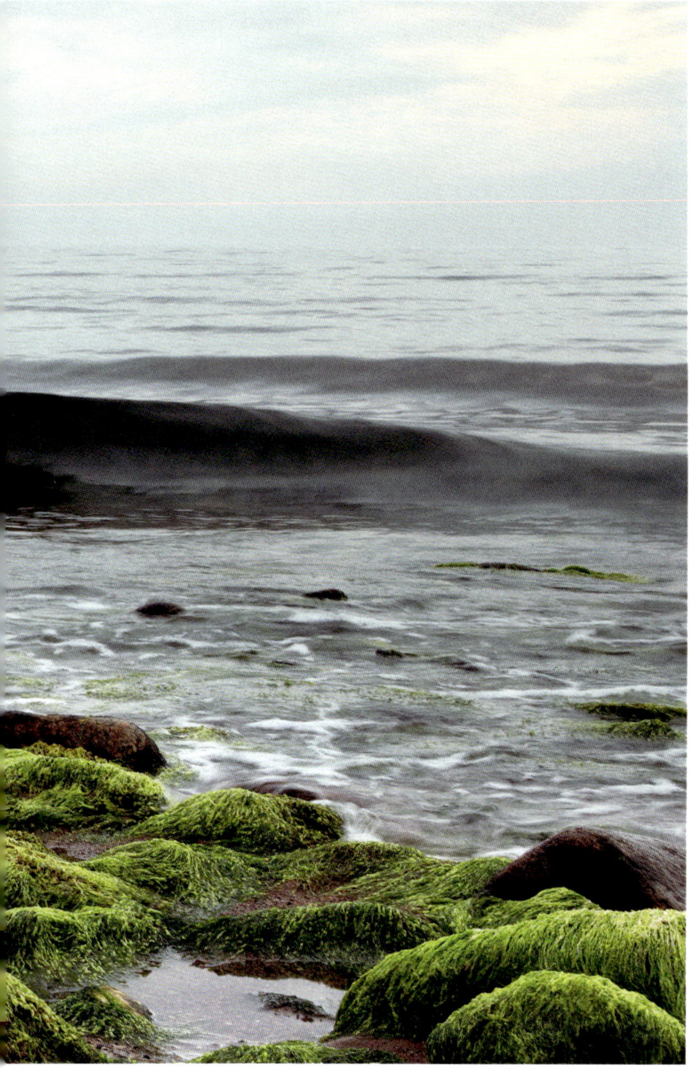

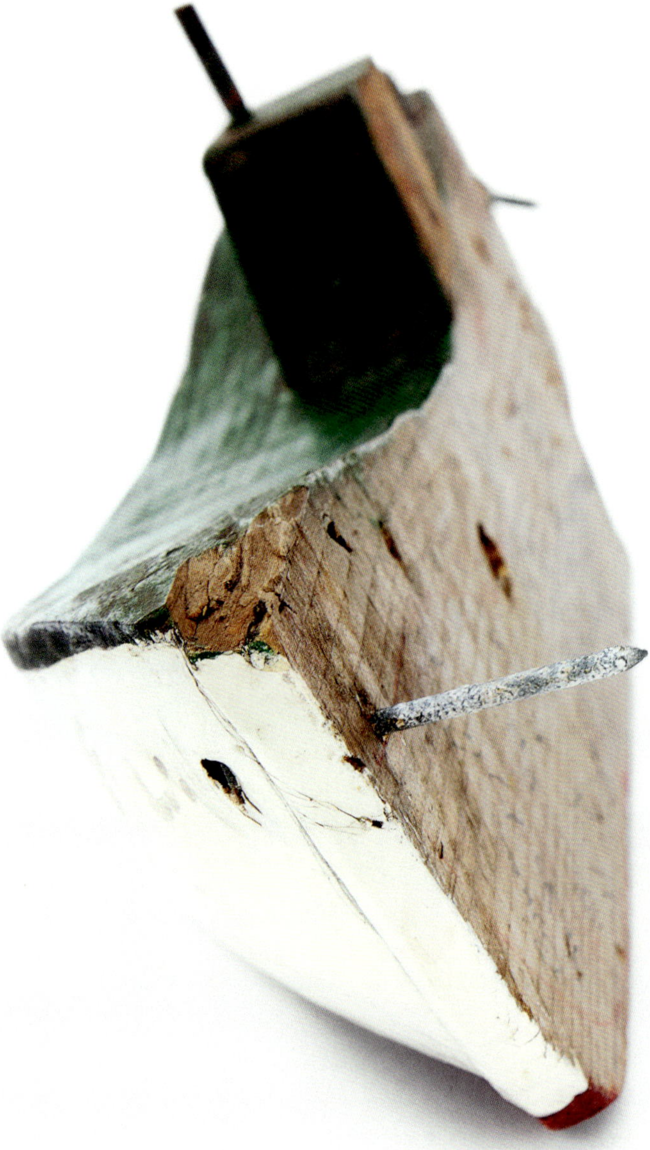

TRAP SKIFF HALF MODEL

Jim Leo Harty, Duntara, Newfoundland and Labrador

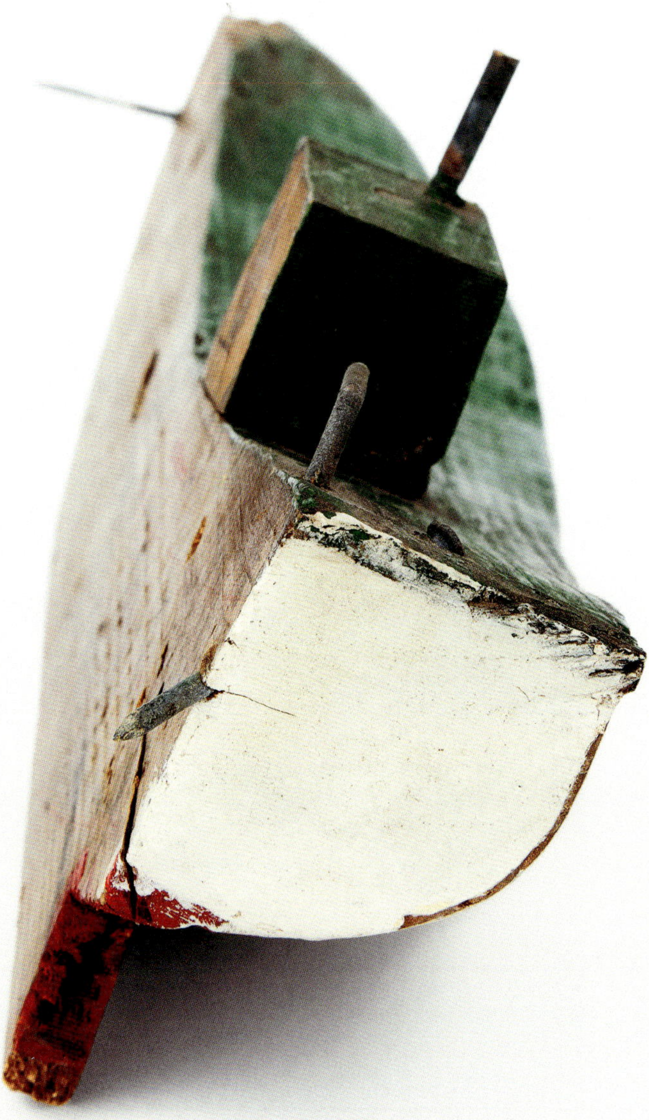

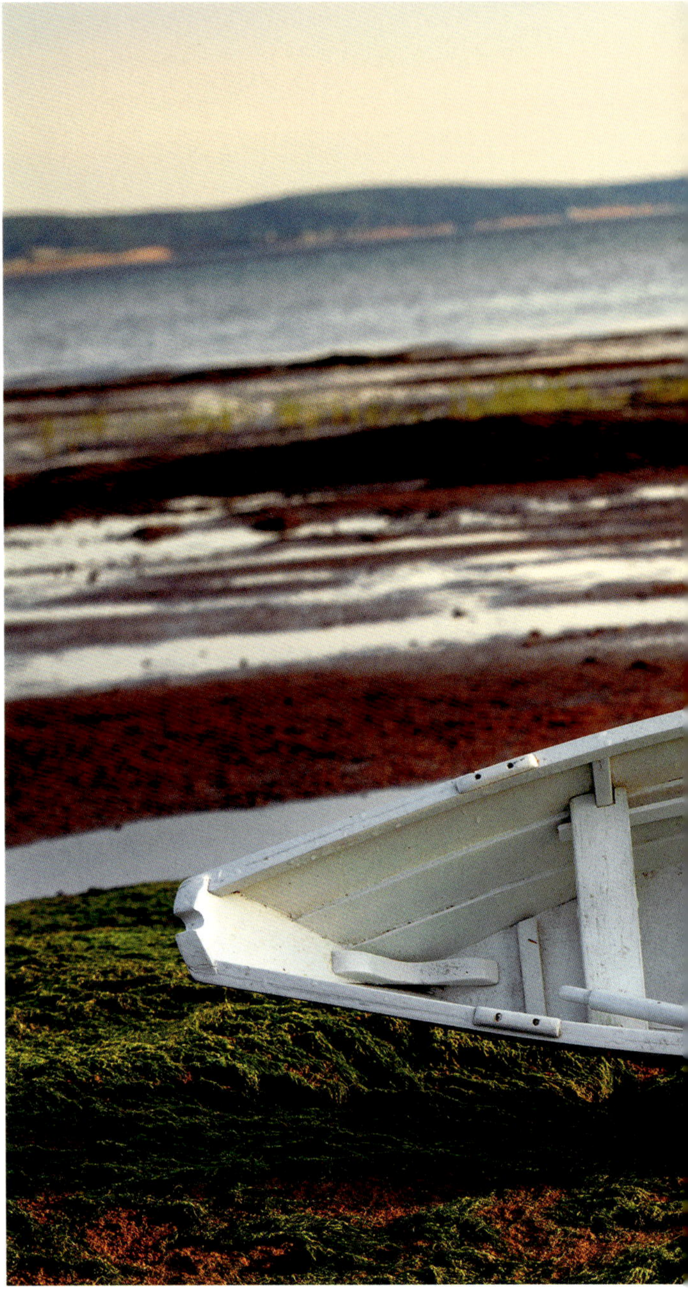

DORY

Maker unknown, Nova Scotia

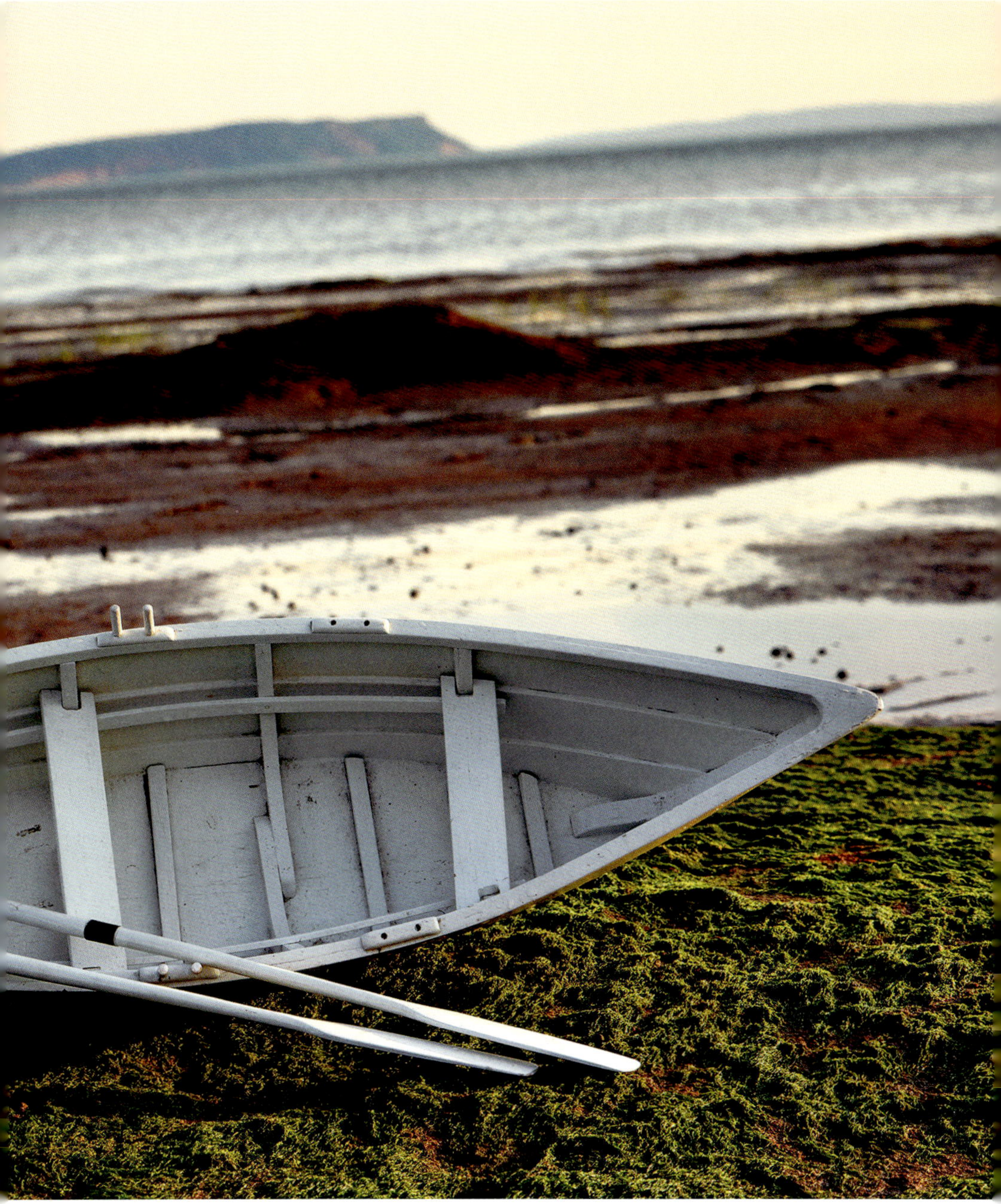

DORY

Maker unknown, Newfoundland and Labrador

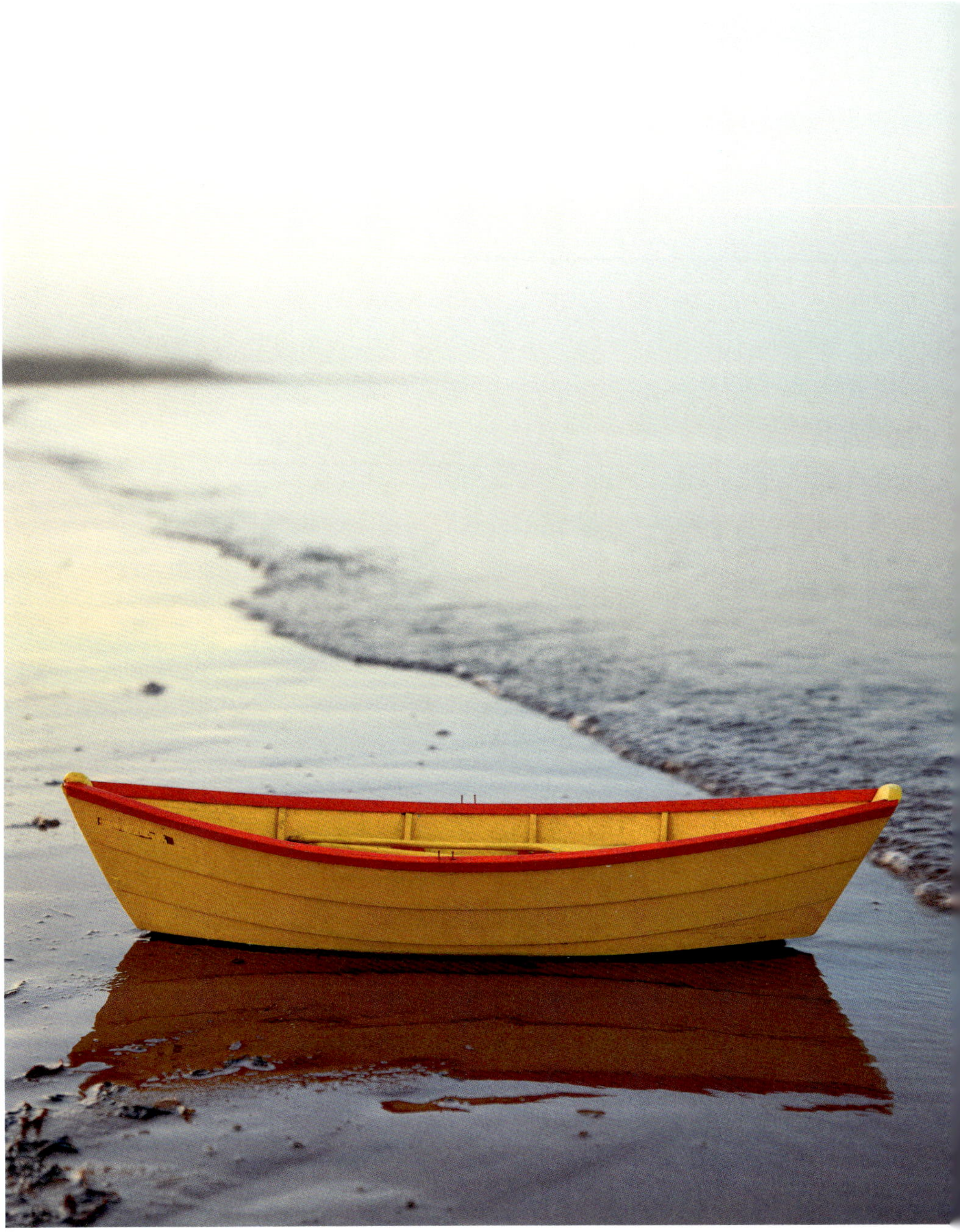

FISHING WAS SUPPOSED TO BE MY LIFE

WATSON KNICKLE
Model Maker

Second Peninsula,
Lunenburg County,
Nova Scotia

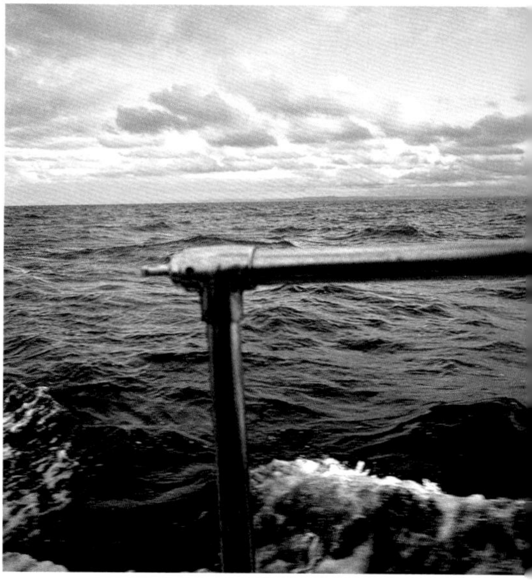

Caribou Harbour, Nova Scotia, 2002

Fishing was supposed to be my life, but it didn't turn out that way. I joined the "Robert-Brian" when I was 16 years old. It was a 65-foot-long liner used for wet fish, haddock, codfish, and swordfish in the summertime. I was with the boat three months, and it is the boat I was shipwrecked on. It was after that I started making models.

When I look at a model boat, I can picture myself in the real boat out to sea, and that gives me the pleasure. I can tell you how long it is, how wide it is, and how deep it should be. I know how fast that boat will go in the water and how good it will perform. I see into things and how they should go together. I make it same as an original would be made, with a keel, a stern, and all planked up. Some are boats that my father owned, or I owned, or boats that I did see that I liked. I don't know if there's such a thing as a perfect boat, but all my boats have a story.

I made a model of the boat I was shipwrecked on. I don't know if I'm proud of it, because it was a terrible experience, but I was happy when I had that finished with the bunks inside, a table and everything. Even though you can't see it, I know it's all there.

It was January 13 or 14, 1959, 30 below Celsius, 1:30 in the morning. We hit a shoal, 89 miles off Isaacs Harbour, up in Guysborough County. The boat took in water. We sent out an SOS to Canso and they sent an SOS to Halifax, but it was too rough to send any boats out and we couldn't get a helicopter because it was snowing and blowing.

The boat started to sink. We went from the wheelhouse up the spar. Then the bottom came out of the boat and the spar went down through the boat. We fell on the wheelhouse. In the meantime, the back of the boat broke apart. We jumped from the wheelhouse to the back of the boat. My dory mates made it. I jumped and I couldn't make it, so I fell in the water, and they pulled me up. We had sort of a raft type of thing, just broken wood from the boat, and we stayed on that, in and out of the water, hanging on.

During that night, my dory mates wanted to let go, and they asked me if I would let go with them. I thought of my family at home, my mother and father and sisters. I said, no, I would not take my own life. So, they hung on. They didn't let go. In the morning, it calmed down, but it was thick of fog. In the meantime, there were two American boats trying to get into Isaacs Harbour. One boat had a broken radar, so they had a man up on the rigging. He looked down and saw us floating around. They stopped and threw a line because they couldn't get too close. We wrapped that line around us and that boat picked us up. It was 9:30 in the morning. We were four aboard and four saved.

I was frozen up bad when they took me onto the dragger. One fella took me by my head, one fella by my leg, I was like a stiff board. I had ice for my body, and all you could see on any of us was our eyeballs and our mouth where we were breathing. We had maybe 15 minutes left to go, and we all would've froze to death.

They had to wait to operate till the gangrene decided where it's going. That was about two months. I had an operation every two weeks and I had 12 operations. The last operation, I asked them when they were going to give an anesthetic and he said, we can't give you one because you had too many for now. So, I had an operation without an anesthetic. I was a while getting over that. Then I started to heal up and things became okay. I spent about eight months in the hospital.

After the accident, I raised a family. I was a draftsman. I did work with the Department of Transport and went up north as a deckhand, and then quartermaster on the HMS "Labrador" icebreaker. In those days when you went up north, you were gone three months. So, I decided to go back to school and upgrade my education. Then I worked in engineering for a hardboard company. I always had a boat. I went out fishing, weekends or that sort of thing.

Model making is one hobby I have. When the finished project is there, you look at it and say, well, it looks good. And then you start thinking of another boat to make, so you just keep on going. You don't spend a whole day at it, you spend just two or three hours and then you leave it and come back and work at it again. I've built well over a hundred model boats. I belonged to the boat model club and there's not many people that are joining. It's a dying out type of thing.

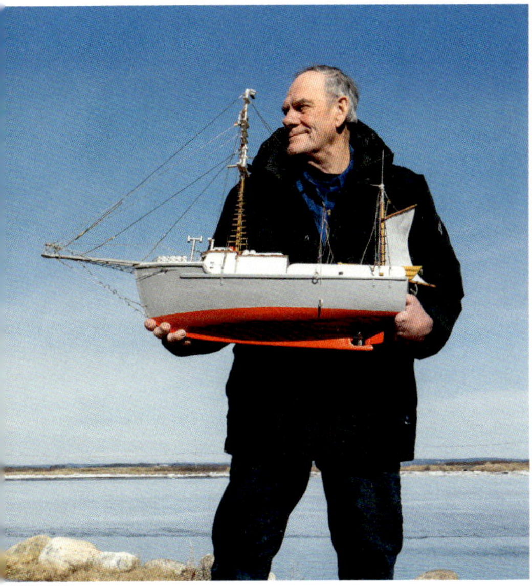

Watson Knickle with the "Robert-Brian," Longliner
Second Peninsula, Nova Scotia

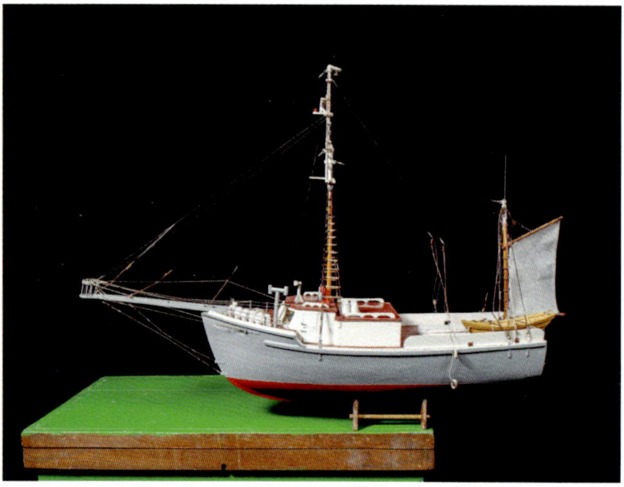

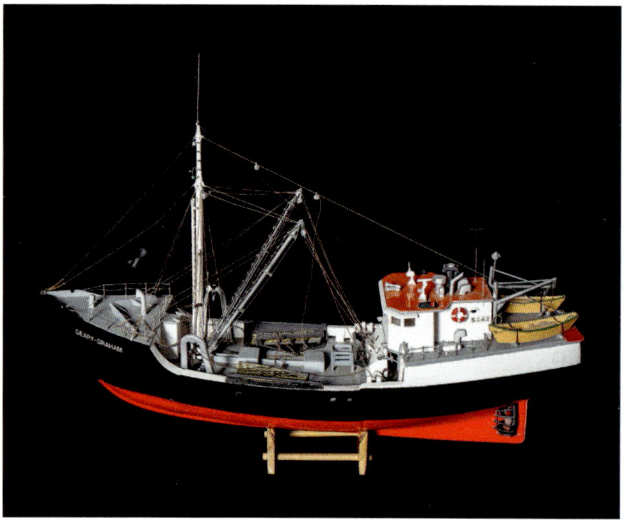

"ROBERT-BRIAN," LONGLINER

Watson Knickle, Second Peninsula, Nova Scotia

"GEARY-GRAHAM," SCALLOP DRAGGER

Watson Knickle, Second Peninsula, Nova Scotia

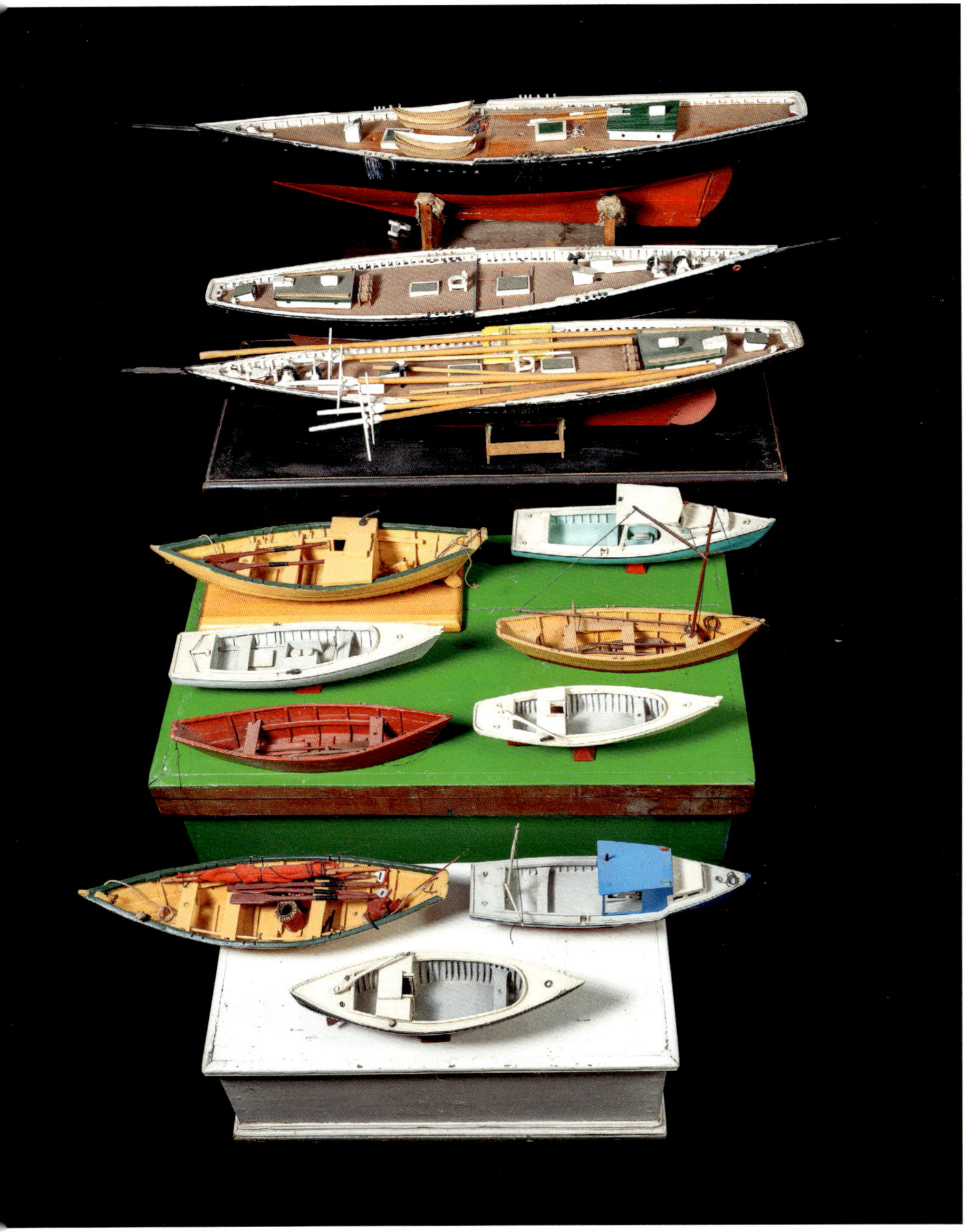

ASSORTED MODELS

Watson Knickle, Second Peninsula, Nova Scotia

"SIR ROBERT BOND," RAILCAR FERRY

Maker unknown, Newfoundland and Labrador

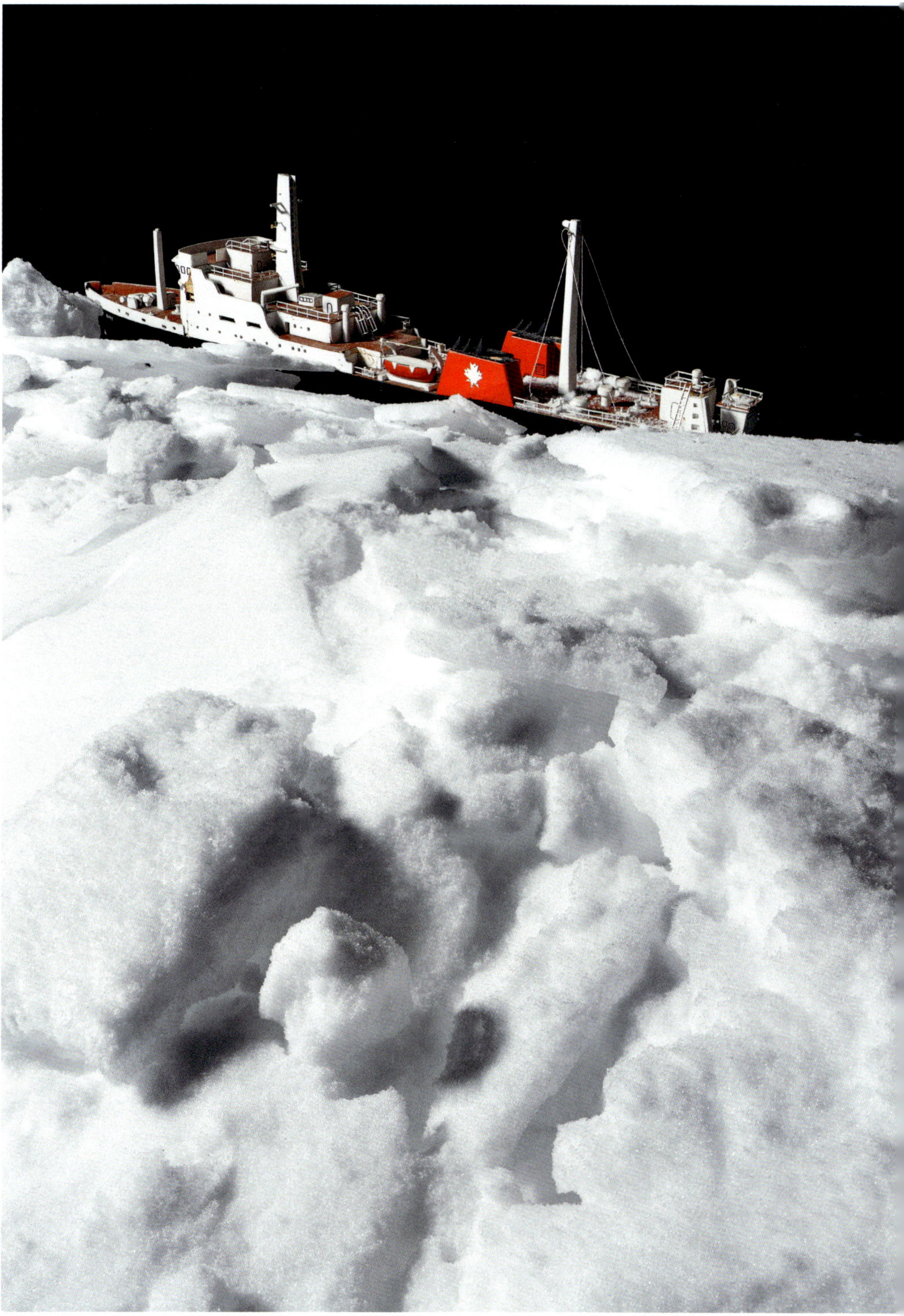

"STEPHANIE KATE," TWO-MASTED SCHOONER

Maker unknown, Newfoundland and Labrador

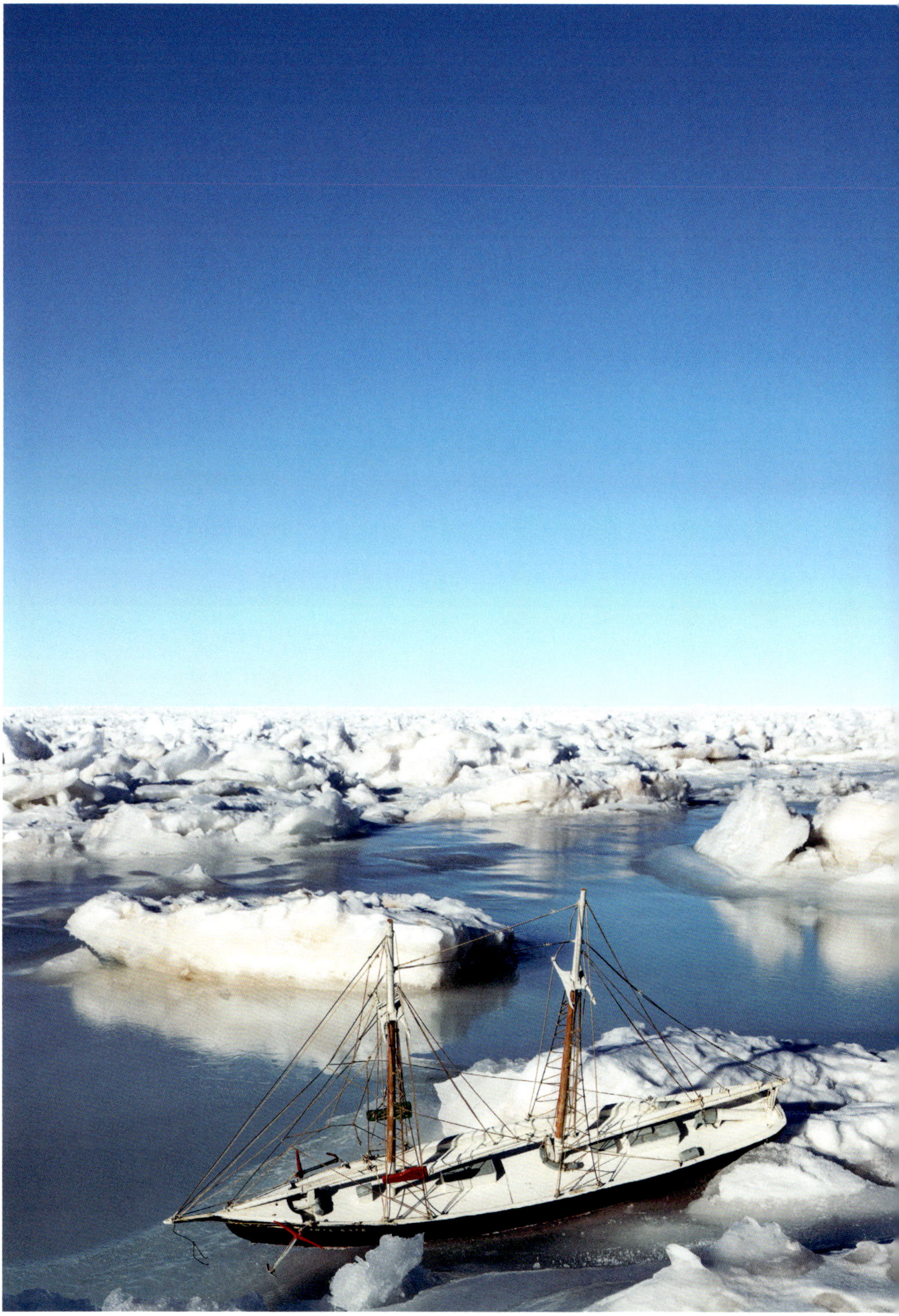

"CHETICAMP," TRAWLER

Maker unknown, Nova Scotia

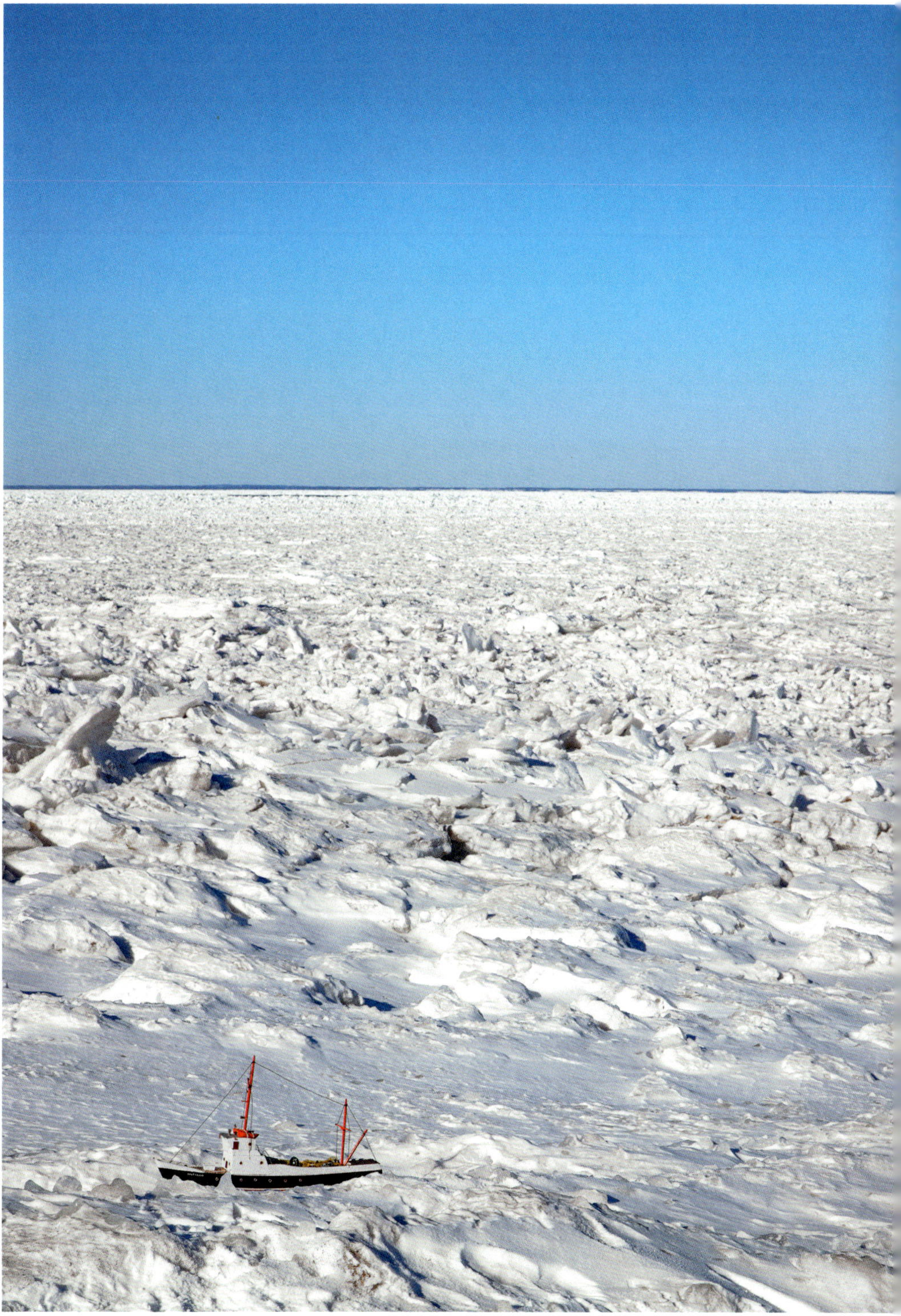

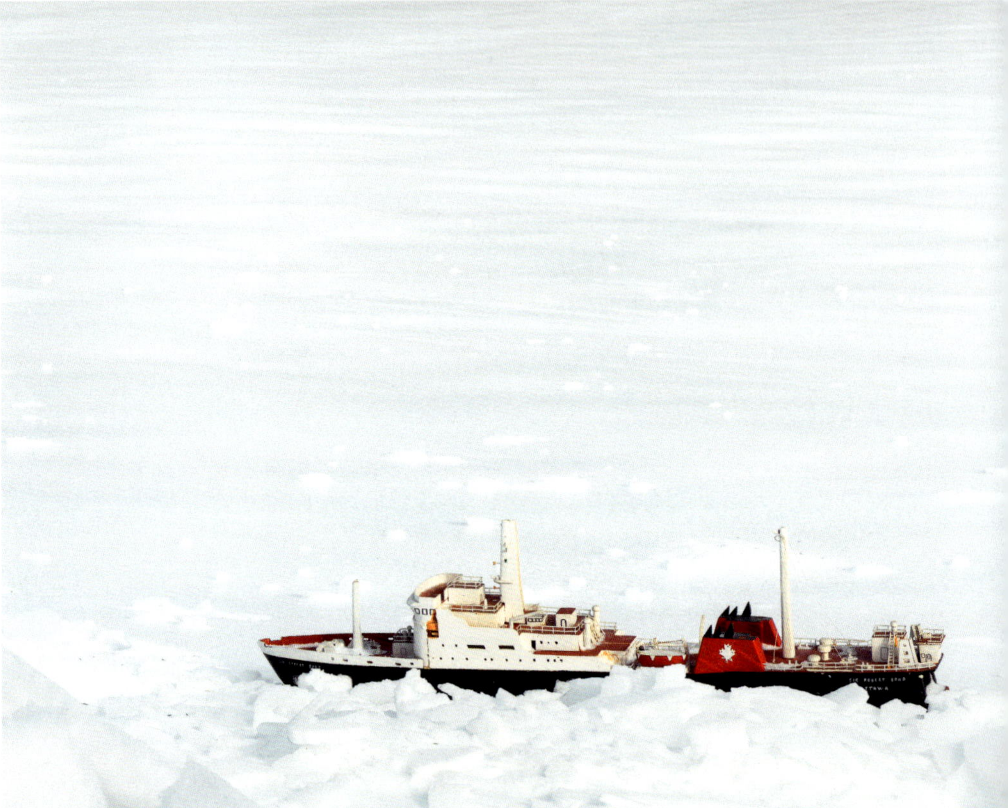

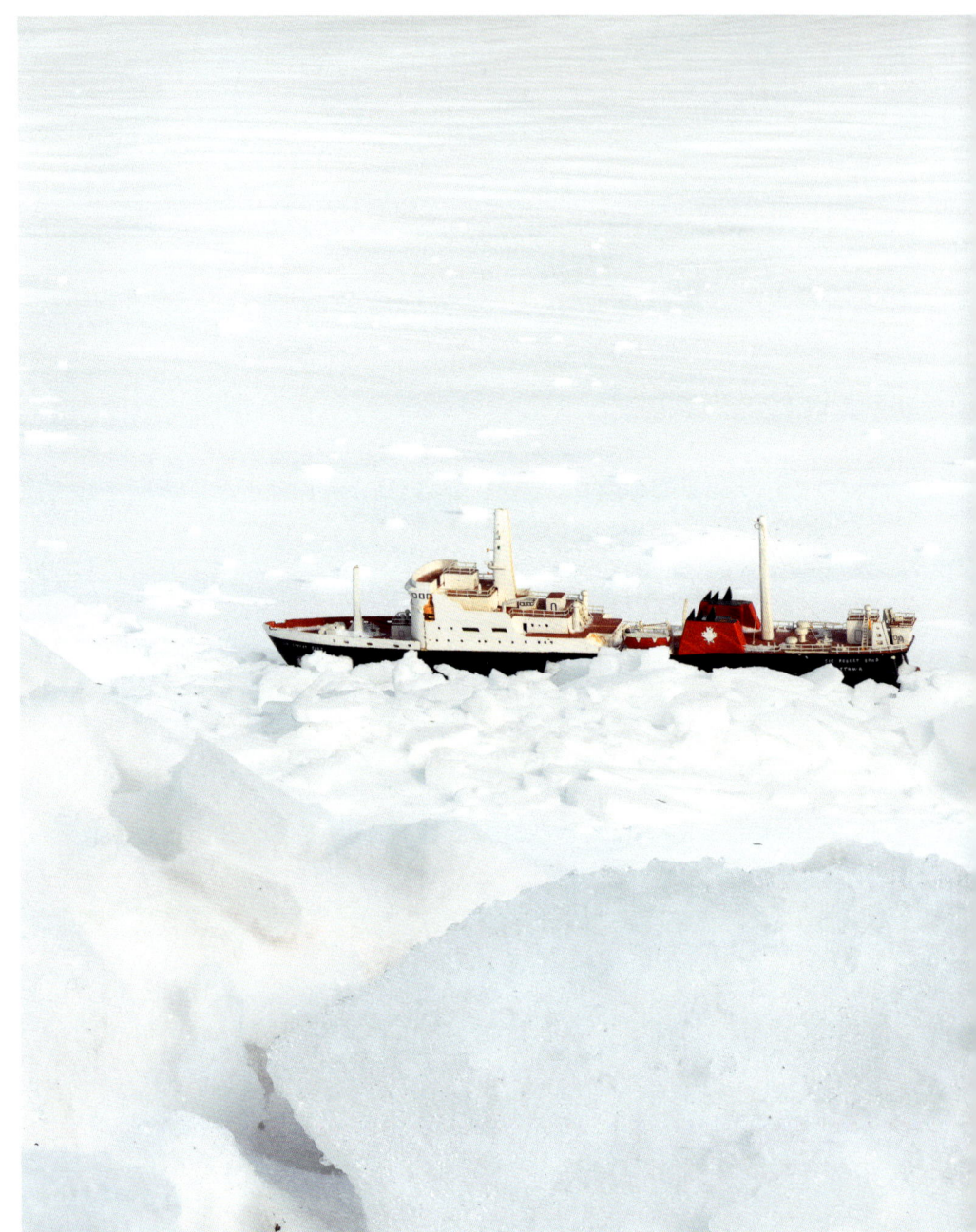

"SIR ROBERT BOND," RAILCAR FERRY

Maker unknown, Newfoundland and Labrador

WE HAD TO KEEP GOING

ROBERT WILKIE

Captain

Painter

Grand River,
Cape Breton Island,
Nova Scotia

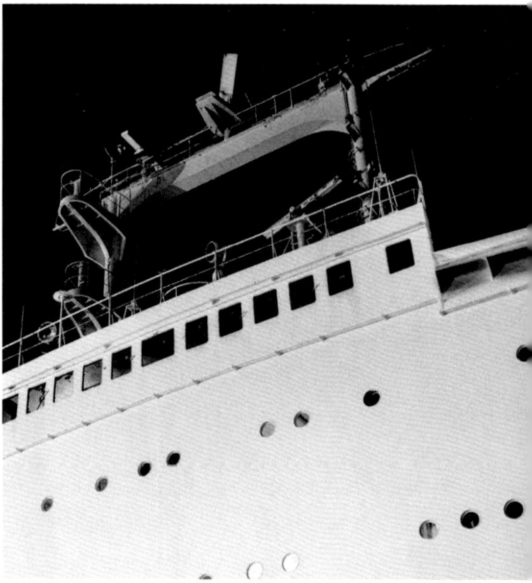

Gulf of St. Lawrence, 2002

Teenagers from North Sydney would get jobs on the ships for the summer. In '71, a bunch of us got hired on as crew on the "Lucy Maud Montgomery" going to Newfoundland, making beds, scrubbing floors. We'd work for two weeks and have two weeks off. I studied art at university in Halifax and then I moved to Montreal. I wasn't making any money on my art and decided to keep going on the ships. I was a deckhand back then and I said, oh, well, if I'm going to be doing this, I may as well get an officer's ticket, be more comfortable, make more money. That was in 1984. I worked as third mate, second mate, but mostly first mate after that. First mate is a big job. You're in charge of loading the boat and managing the deck crew.

I did a lot of training by book. But I did go on a ship-handling course to England that used model boats. I would say the models were about 15 to 20 feet long. And they were long enough for two of us, one to be captain and the other engineer. You weren't in a bridge. You were sitting in the open, like a canoe basically, only it was motorized, had rudders, and handled the way a big ship would handle. We took turns. There were probably about eight or nine boats, different models, tankers and passenger ships, on this small, manmade lake, just deep enough for these boats to move around. There were canals built into it, anchorages and things like that, and we were interacting with other vessels. It was training and decision-making in real time on model ships.

I was 25 years with Marine Atlantic going around Newfoundland and up north to Labrador. I was on the ferries, and the last five years I was on the coastal boats delivering passengers and freight. It was great! In Labrador, the whole community would come down when you docked. If there was no wharf, we would anchor, and the fishermen would come along the ship and we'd lower freight down onto their boats with our deck crane. When

I got my captain's ticket in the early '90s, I didn't stay with Marine Atlantic, I went up in the Great Lakes.

When I first went on a ship, it was all the radar, cathode ray tube radar. Some nights in Labrador, you were constantly running from the radar to the chart table and then back to piloting the ship. The seas were deep and the waves high. When there was a storm, you'd see rocks that were normally submerged coming to the surface. We called them sunkers. Once in the Cabot Strait we were 45 days straight in fog. Now everything is done by GPS. You have a GPS that gives you your position all the time, and you have electronic charts that show your ship travelling across the surface of the earth, and the depths of the water and everything. It's the idea of floating through the water, being on the move all the time.

Crews do safety drills. Everyone needs to know their duties and responsibilities. I was on the "Jarl Transporter," a Swedish vessel chartered by Marine Atlantic, when we had to cut some freight loose. The "Jarl" was what we call a stiff ship. It was terrible. It would roll out and then whack back again, coming back to its centre fast with a jerky roll. There was a big swell on the water and we were carrying piggybacks—the big trailers used in trucking. One of the trailers came loose from its chains, and it was moving three feet one way and back three feet the other way. We tried three times to hook the chain on the piggyback's chassis. We were kneeling right under it. It was crazy! The mate called the captain and he told us to knock off all its chains. The captain turned the ship and the piggyback went over the side. We called the Coast Guard and gave position. The moon was full and it was shining down on this piggyback trailer upside down, with its wheels spinning right next to the ship. We had to keep going.

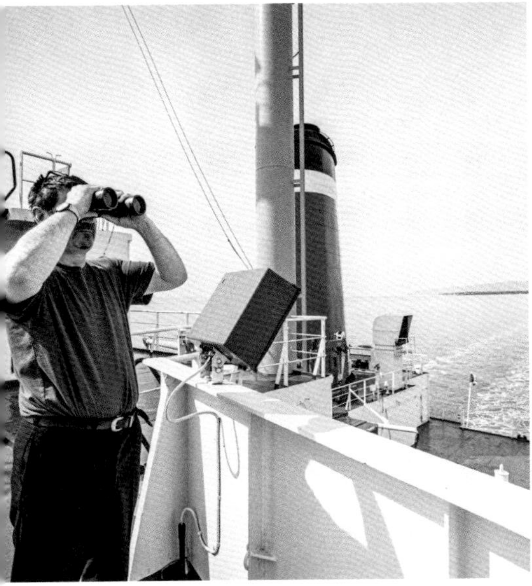

Gulf of St. Lawrence, 2002

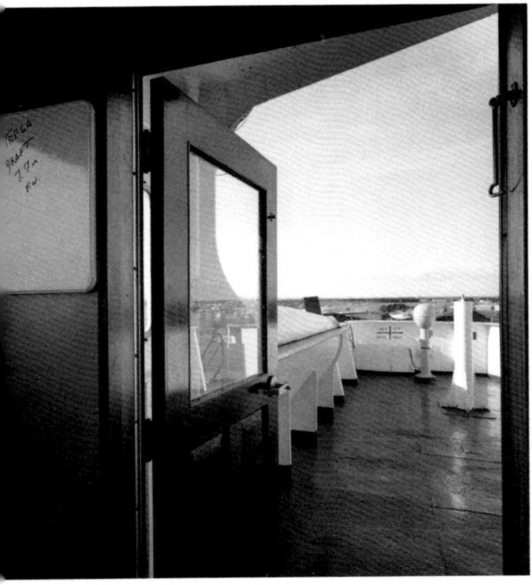

Gulf of St. Lawrence, 2002

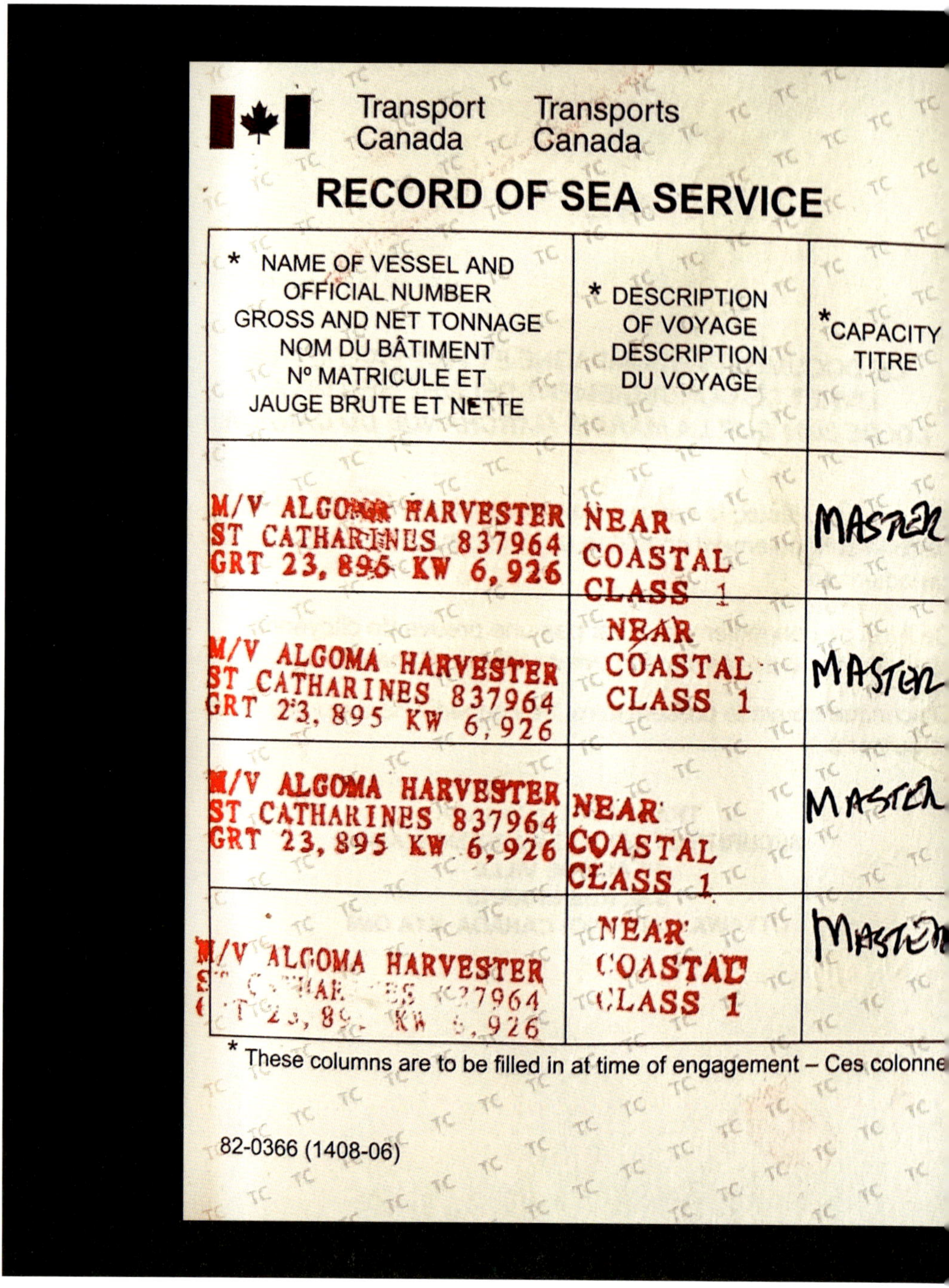

Transport Canada Transports Canada

RECORD OF SEA SERVICE

* NAME OF VESSEL AND OFFICIAL NUMBER GROSS AND NET TONNAGE NOM DU BÂTIMENT Nº MATRICULE ET JAUGE BRUTE ET NETTE	* DESCRIPTION OF VOYAGE DESCRIPTION DU VOYAGE	*CAPACITY TITRE
M/V ALGOMA HARVESTER ST CATHARINES 837964 GRT 23,895 KW 6,926	NEAR COASTAL CLASS 1	MASTER
M/V ALGOMA HARVESTER ST CATHARINES 837964 GRT 23,895 KW 6,926	NEAR COASTAL CLASS 1	MASTER
M/V ALGOMA HARVESTER ST CATHARINES 837964 GRT 23,895 KW 6,926	NEAR COASTAL CLASS 1	MASTER
M/V ALGOMA HARVESTER S[illegible] C[illegible]HAR[illegible]ES [illegible]7964 [illegible]T 23,89[illegible] KW [illegible],926	NEAR COASTAL CLASS 1	MASTER

* These columns are to be filled in at time of engagement – Ces colonne

82-0366 (1408-06)

Robert Wilkie, Record of Sea Service, August 2023–August 2024, Discharge Book, Department of Transport, Canada.

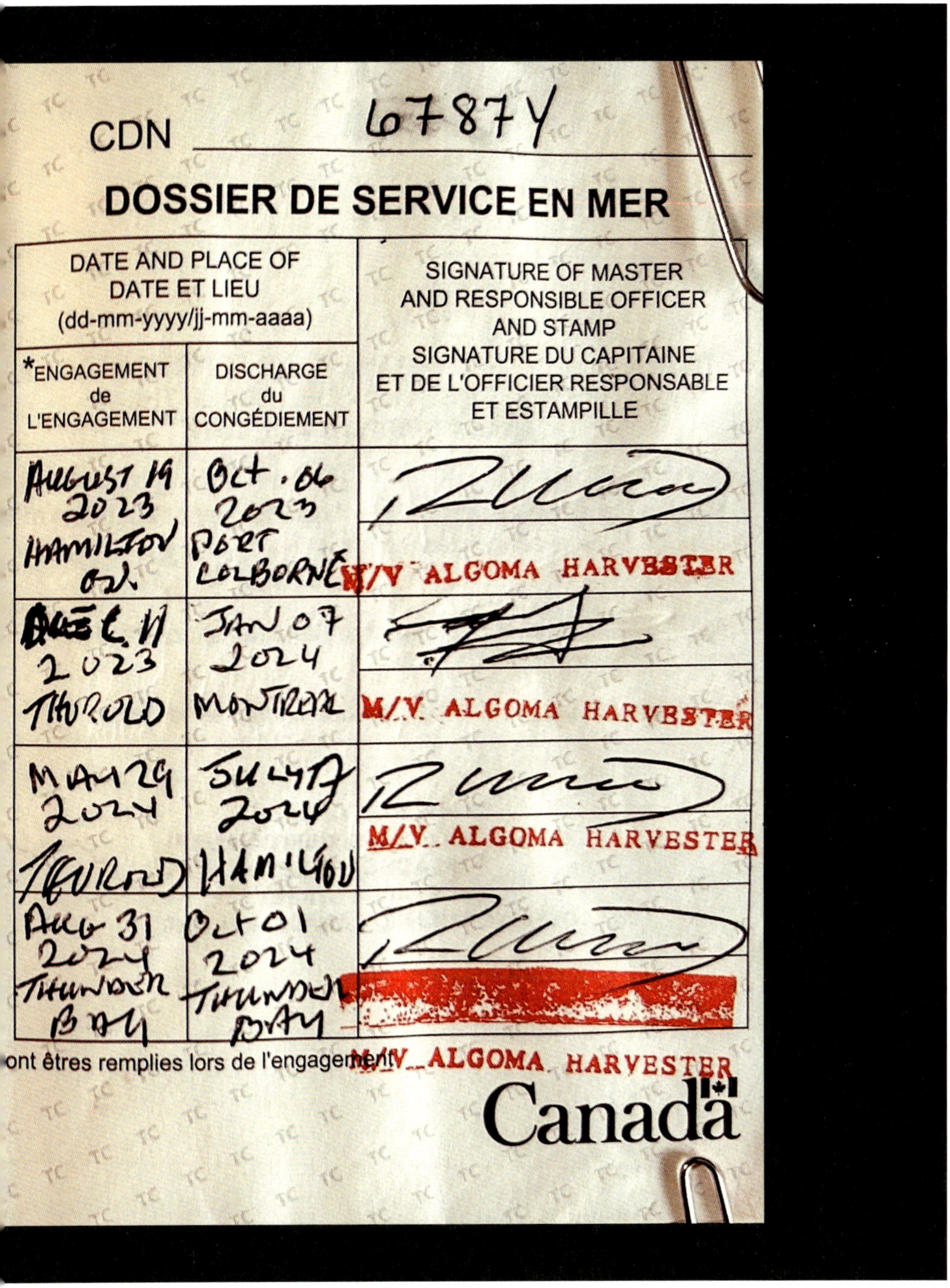

CDN 67874

DOSSIER DE SERVICE EN MER

DATE AND PLACE OF DATE ET LIEU (dd-mm-yyyy/jj-mm-aaaa)		SIGNATURE OF MASTER AND RESPONSIBLE OFFICER AND STAMP SIGNATURE DU CAPITAINE ET DE L'OFFICIER RESPONSABLE ET ESTAMPILLE
*ENGAGEMENT de L'ENGAGEMENT	DISCHARGE du CONGÉDIEMENT	
AUGUST 19 2023 HAMILTON ON.	Oct. 06 2023 PORT COLBORNE	M/V ALGOMA HARVESTER
AUG. 11 2023 THOROLD	JAN 07 2024 MONTREAL	M/V ALGOMA HARVESTER
MAY 29 2024 THOROLD	JULY 17 2024 HAMILTON	M/V ALGOMA HARVESTER
AUG 31 2024 THUNDER BAY	OCT 01 2024 THUNDER BAY	

ont êtres remplies lors de l'engagement

M/V ALGOMA HARVESTER

Canada

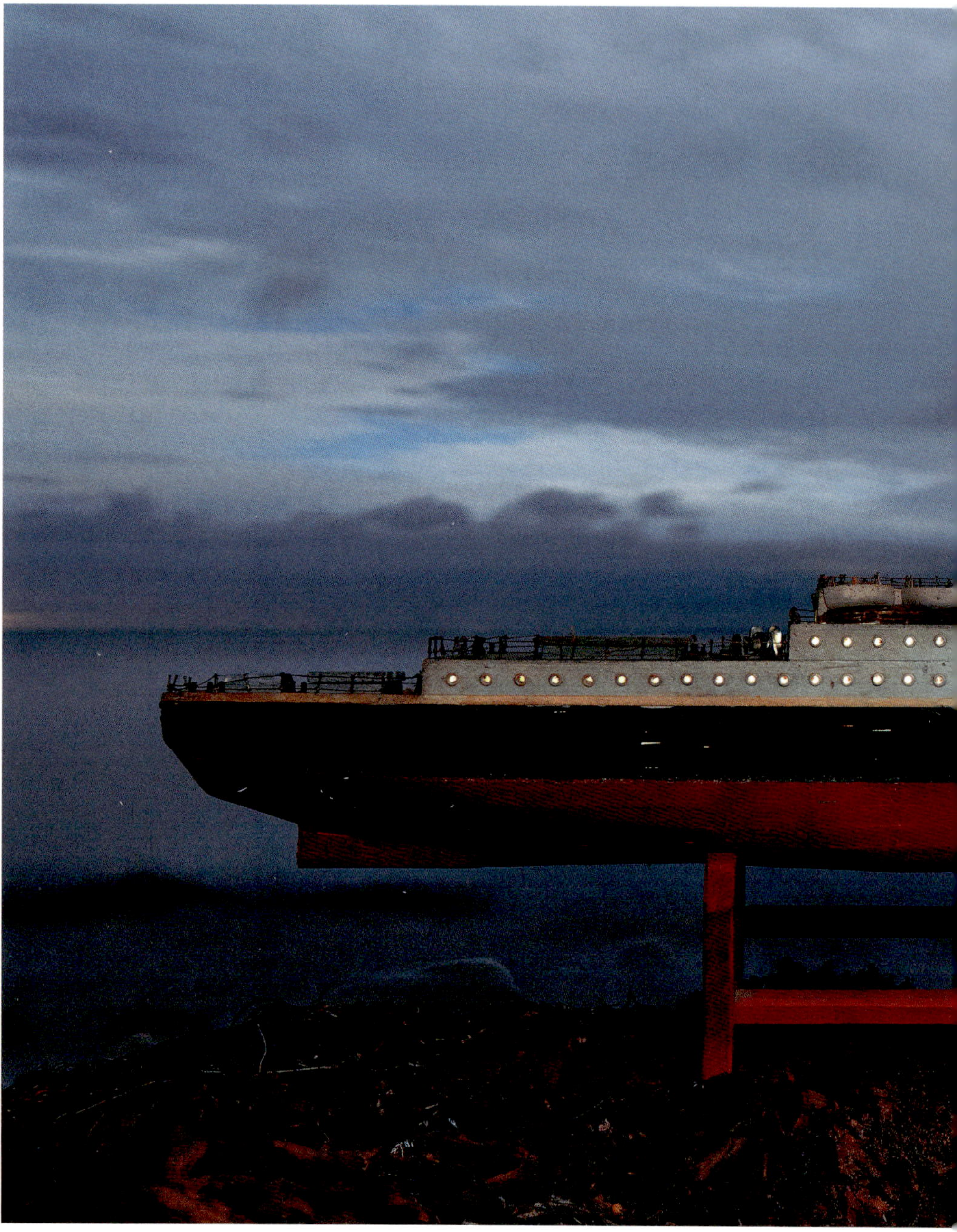

"SS AMERICA," OCEAN LINER

Maker unknown, Nova Scotia

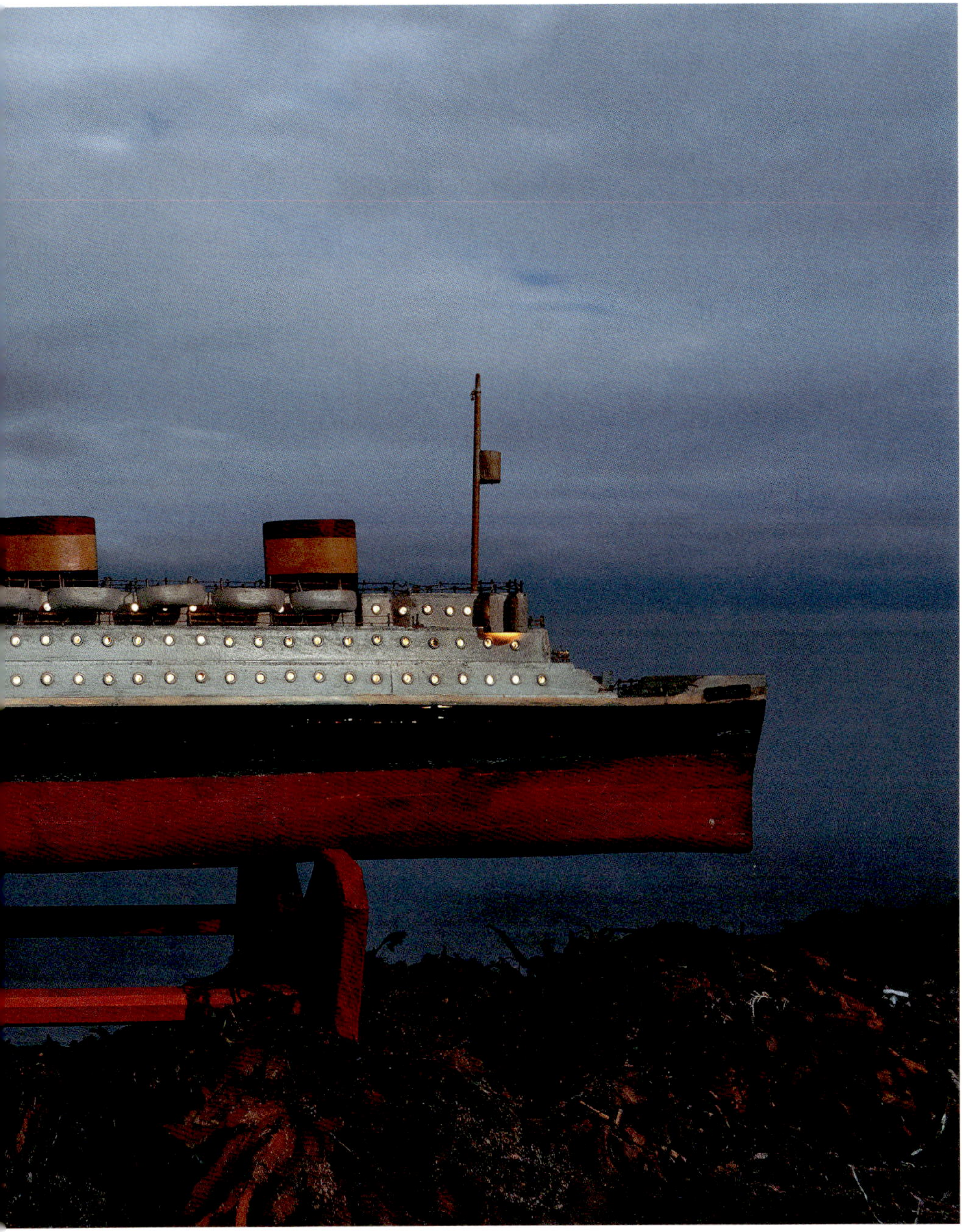

COASTAL BOAT

Maker unknown, Nova Scotia

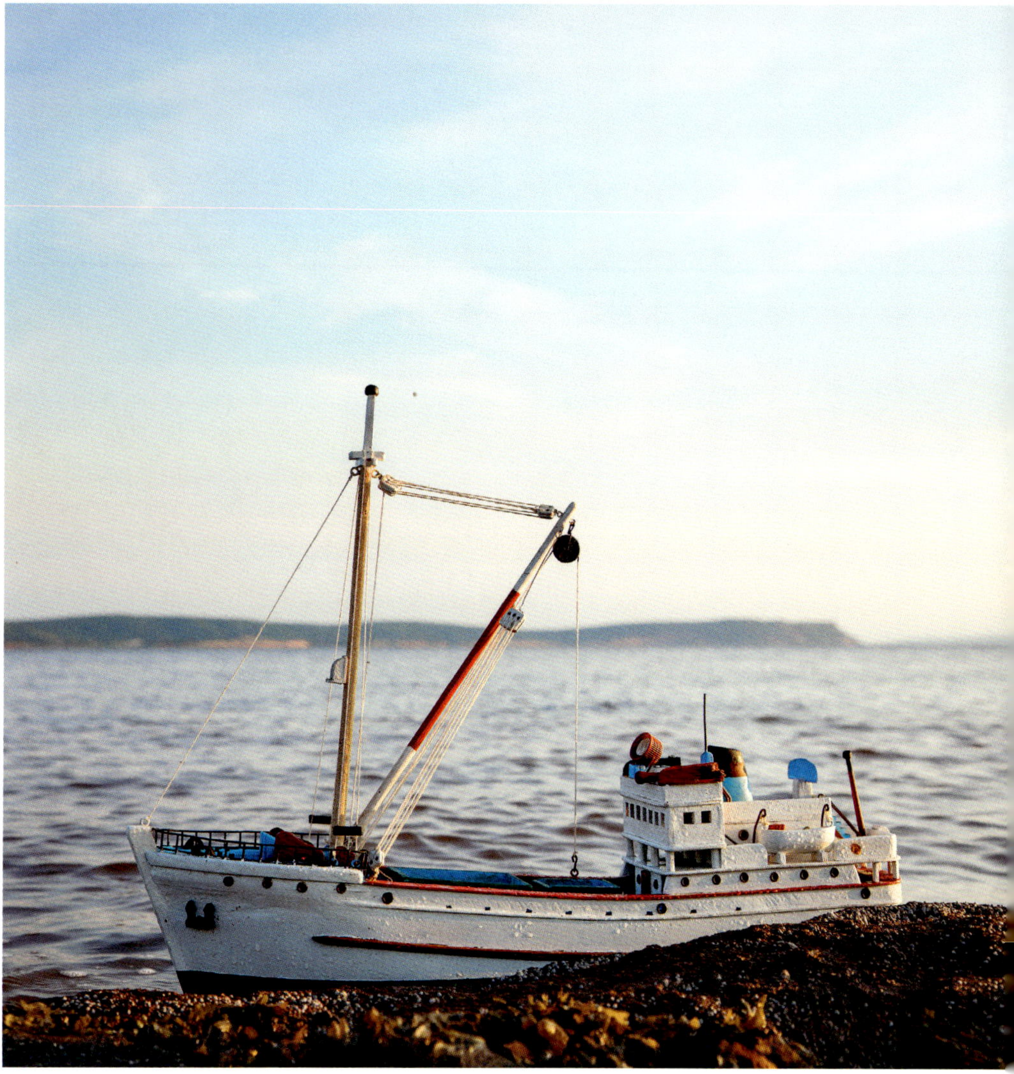

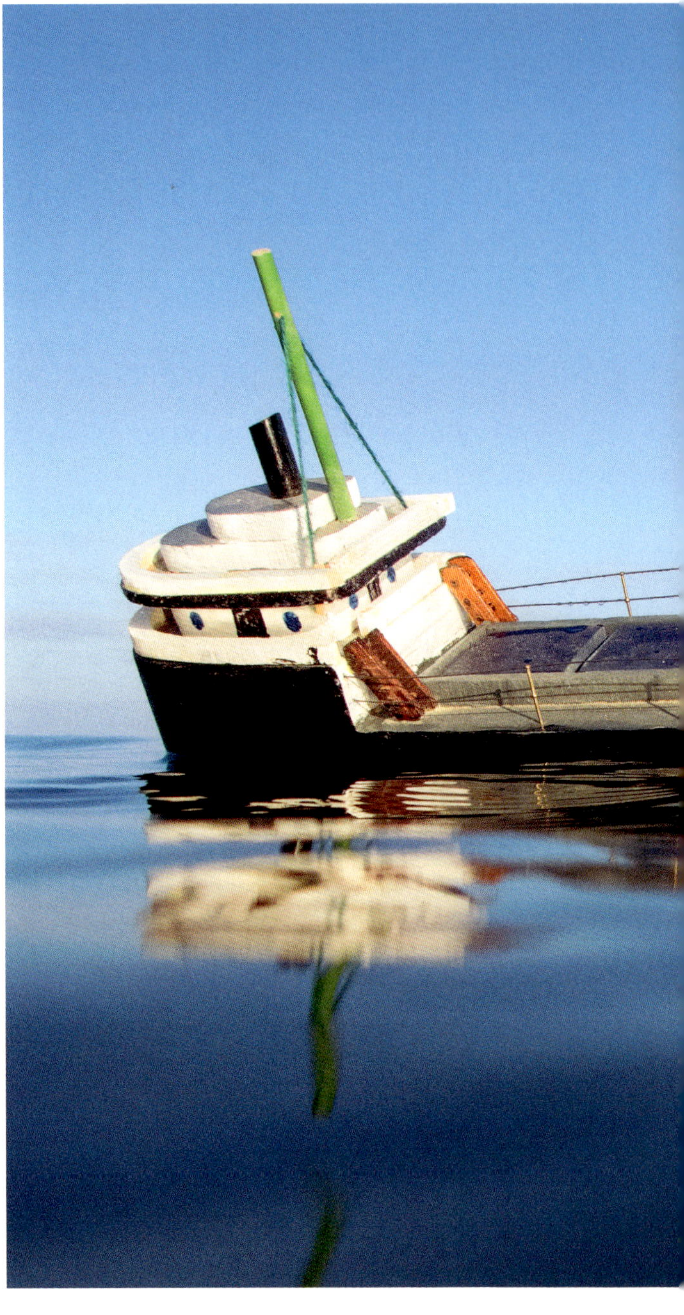

LAKE FREIGHTER

Carson Welch, Newcombville, Nova Scotia

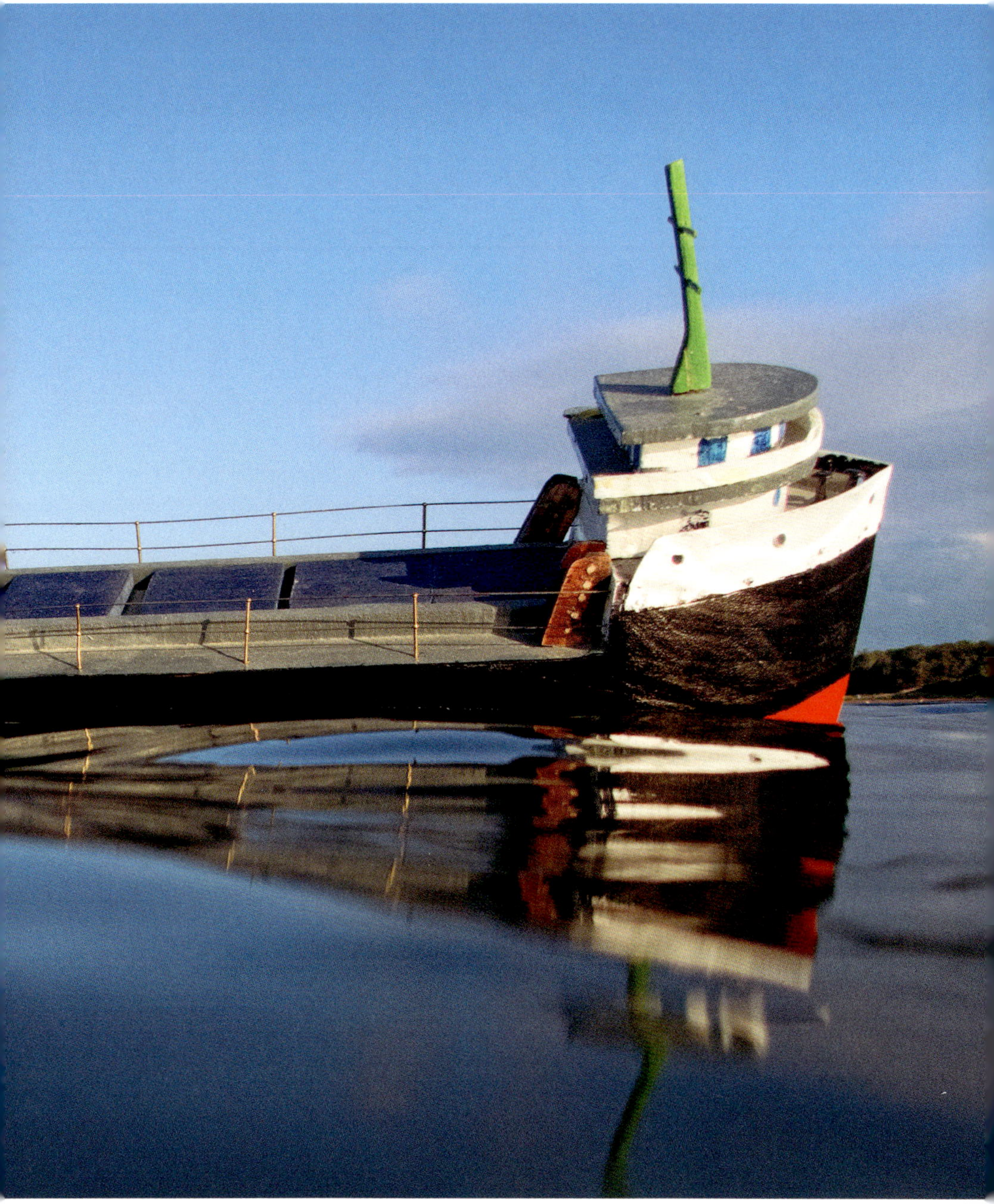

SIDE TRAWLER

Maker unknown, Nova Scotia

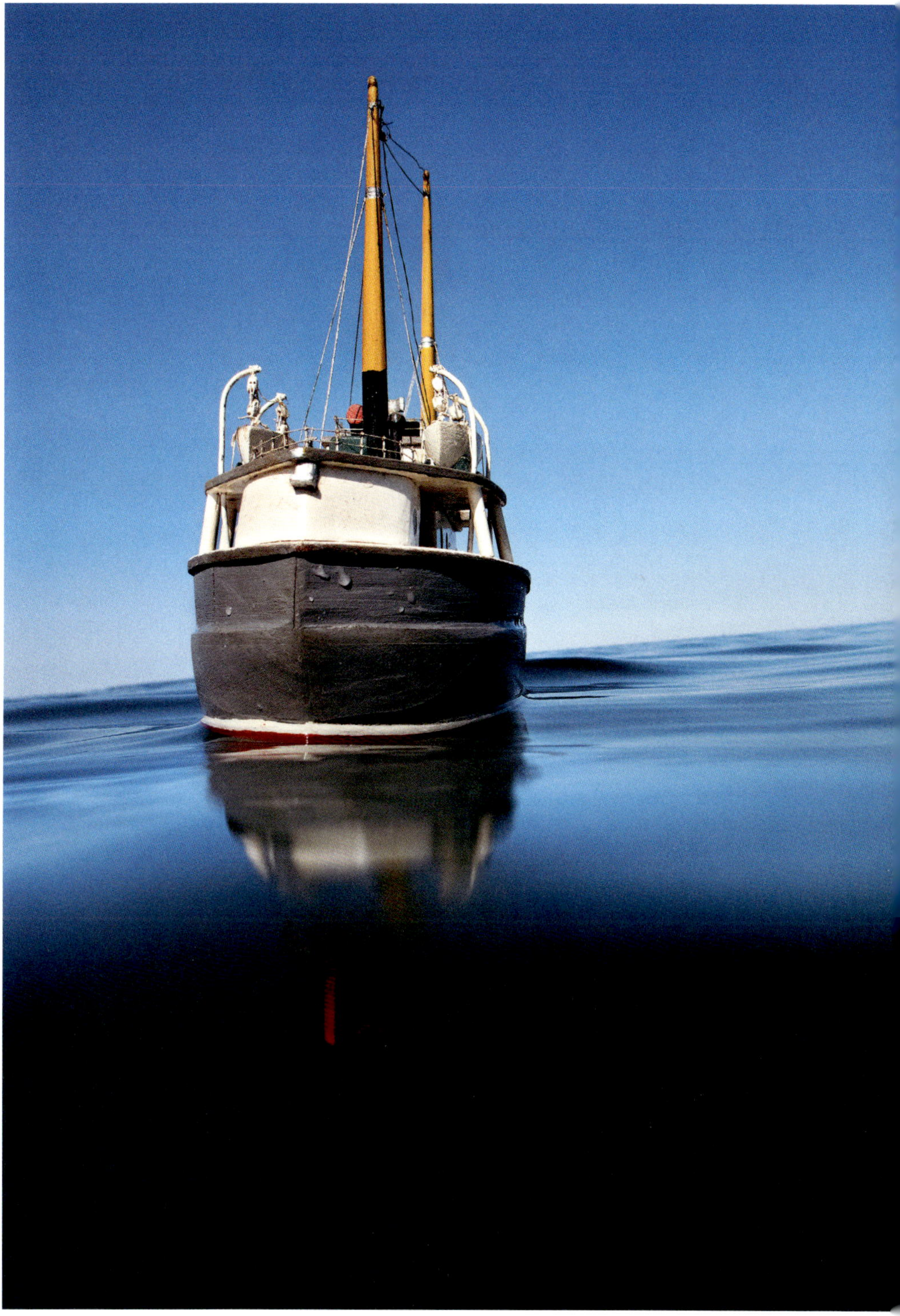

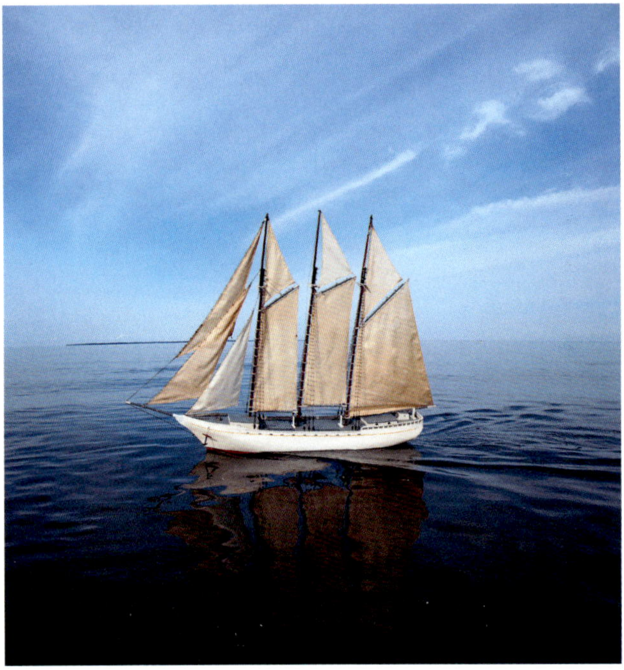

THREE-MASTED SCHOONER

Maker unknown, Nova Scotia

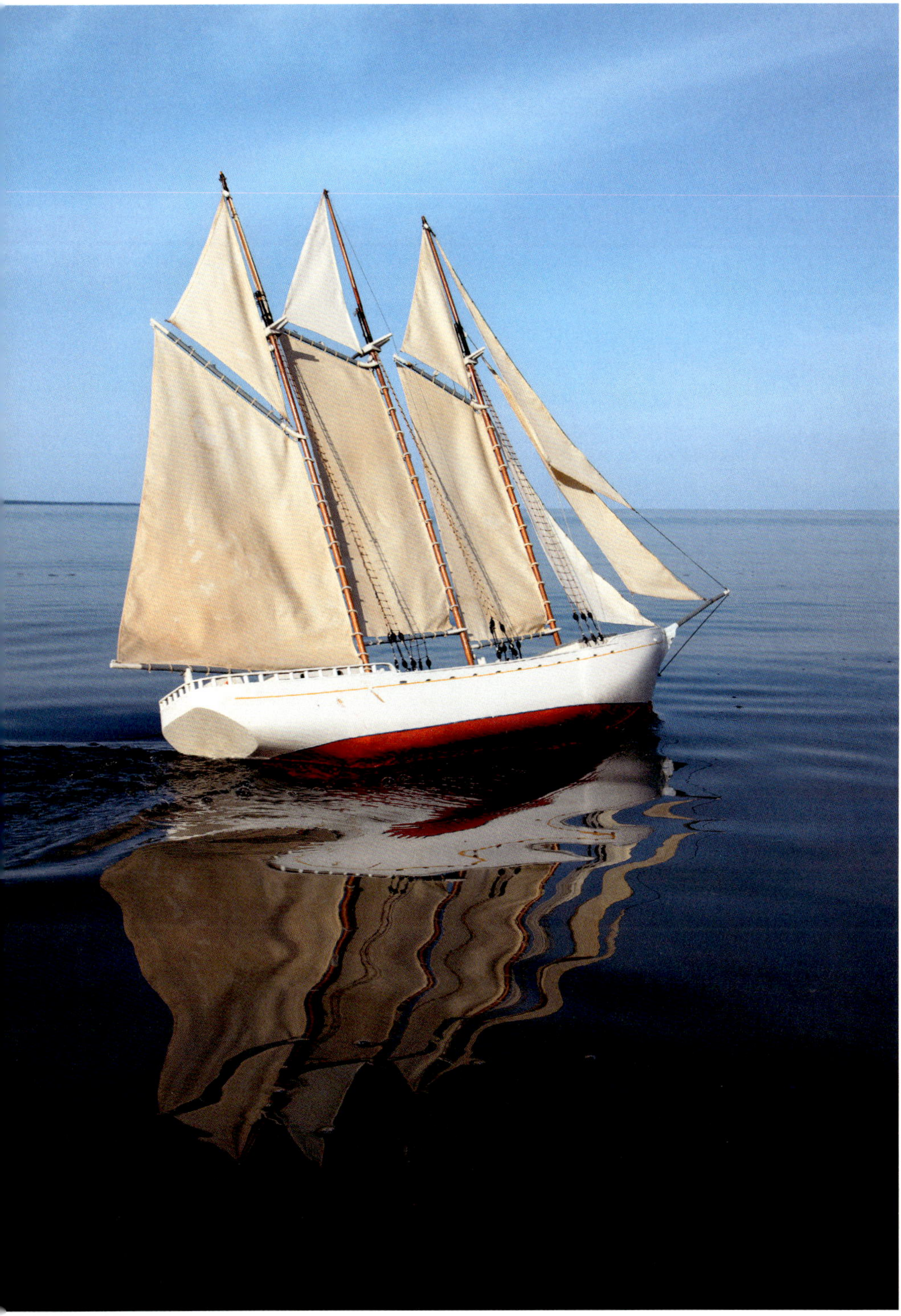

WATER AND WEATHER

SARA SPIKE
Cultural Historian

Jeddore Oyster Pond,
Halifax County,
Nova Scotia

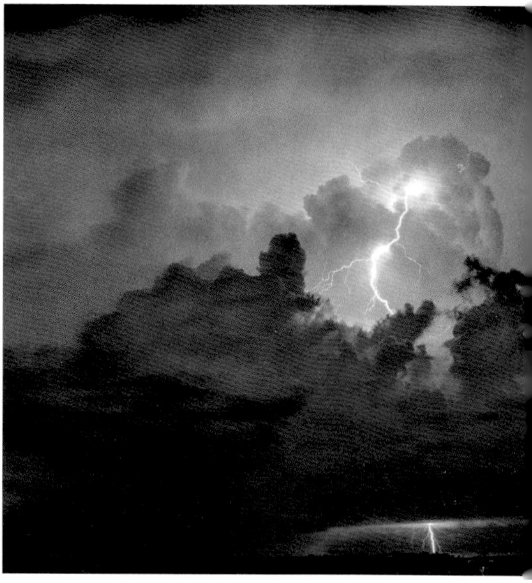

Caribou Harbour, Nova Scotia, 2015

Coastal communities are shaped by the rhythms of water and weather. The eternal tides are a marker of hours, tied to the moon, ebbing and flowing twice a day, exposing a foreshore of chance and change. The annual cycle of the seasons brings a familiar round of sensory and emotional encounters, less predictable today than one hundred years ago, but still reassuringly routine. Weather systems punctuate these patterns with the drama of violent storms and the quiet melancholy of grey. Sky, water, ice, fog.

Coastal people have always been weather watchers. Mackerel skies, mares' tails, red sky at night: sailor's delight. These folk traditions of weather prediction have a counterpart in the careful documentation of weather that has come to pass. In petroglyphs, stories, journals, daybooks and diaries, logbooks, and official records, generations of weather watchers have carefully observed the sky and described the daily relationship between atmosphere and ocean along the coast. Many of these documents are now held by historical archives, or treasured as family heirlooms.

Logbooks of ships that visited the coasts of Atlantic Canada are some of the earliest records of daily weather watching in the region. Often hours, days, weeks on end of thick fog veiling the coast baffled and frustrated mariners. The lifting of these mists was cause for celebration as wet sails were unreefed and a ship began to glide once more over the dark ocean toward St. John's or Halifax or some harbour somewhere. The Mi'kmaq also keep memories of historical fogs, notably those that gave their name to the island of Cape Breton: Unama'ki, land of fog.

Beginning in the early 19th century, colonial governments enlisted thousands of residents to document daily weather conditions for the early meteorological service that would eventually become Environment Canada. In addition to notes about temperatures and cloud cover, these volunteers described their observations of seasonal changes, notable weather events, and other details that caught their eye or their imagination. Likewise, schoolchildren and teachers across early 20th-century Nova Scotia recorded the appearance of wildflowers and migrating birds for an elaborate nature-study project run by the Department of Education. Those along the coast took the opportunity to remark upon local details such as the first ship in port and the first catch of haddock in the spring. Employees of the Canadian lighthouse service were issued journals to keep track of how many hours a day their lamps were illuminated, varying greatly from the darkest days of winter to the early mornings and late evenings of summer. They also noted how many days a month their groaning foghorn bellowed out its call through thick weather to passing ships. Notations were typically brief: Fair, Overcast, Fog. But they give a sense of the intimate familiarity with weather that was commonplace for these caretakers at the farthest reaches of land into sea.

For women and men keeping personal diaries in rural communities, the weather was part of the story of their day, often shaping how they spent their time. Snow, rain, or warm summer days were noted alongside descriptions of labour and leisure, sowing and harvesting, visits with friends, hauling seaweed from the shore, church services and pie socials, chopping wood, drying cod, quilting bees, the first spring peepers, the first hard frost, the highest tide for years.

In the 19th century, the reliable cold of winter froze harbours solid, catching and holding ships in an icy grip until spring brought a thaw to release them. Those warm days were greeted by fragrant pink mayflowers blooming at the edge of the woods, and air full of birdsong, white-throated sparrows, black-capped chickadees, red-breasted robins. At the coast, summer was blue upon blue, water and sky, and enormous fluffy clouds, but also the arrival of

Old Grey Face, the familiar though never welcome bank of fog that enshrouded many harbours and bays for hours or days at a time. August gales and autumn storms marked the shifting of the seasons once again, and soon the skies filled with wild geese in skeins pointing south, stopping to rest and feed on saltmarsh grasses and fields of aftermath.

Today's weather watchers know that this cycle continues but with perceptible changes. Harbours rarely freeze so hard, storms are wilder, the geese have altered their route. What remains is weather and water, ebb and flow, and watching. Weather is a constant topic of conversation in coastal communities, a source of frustrations and joy. The weather, like the seasons and the tides, is lived-in, well worn, well known, a character in coastal places throughout Atlantic Canada, today as in the past.

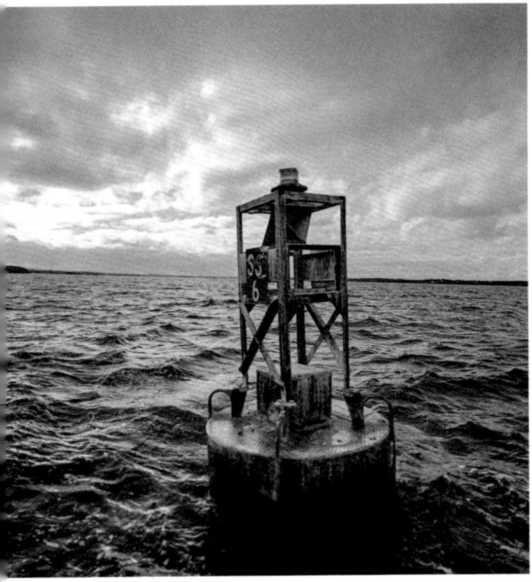

Caribou Harbour, 2002

BARQUE

Maker unknown, Nova Scotia

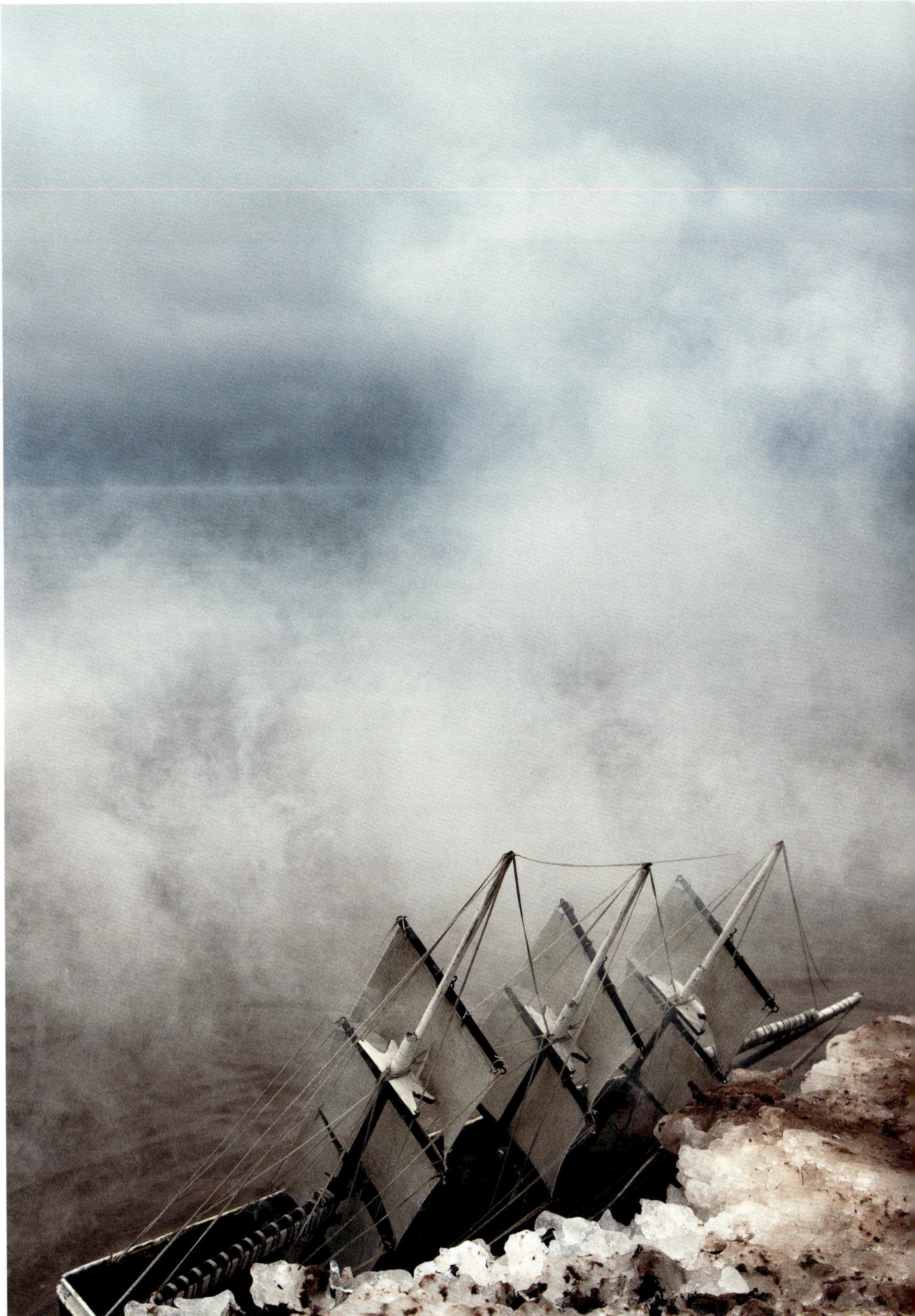

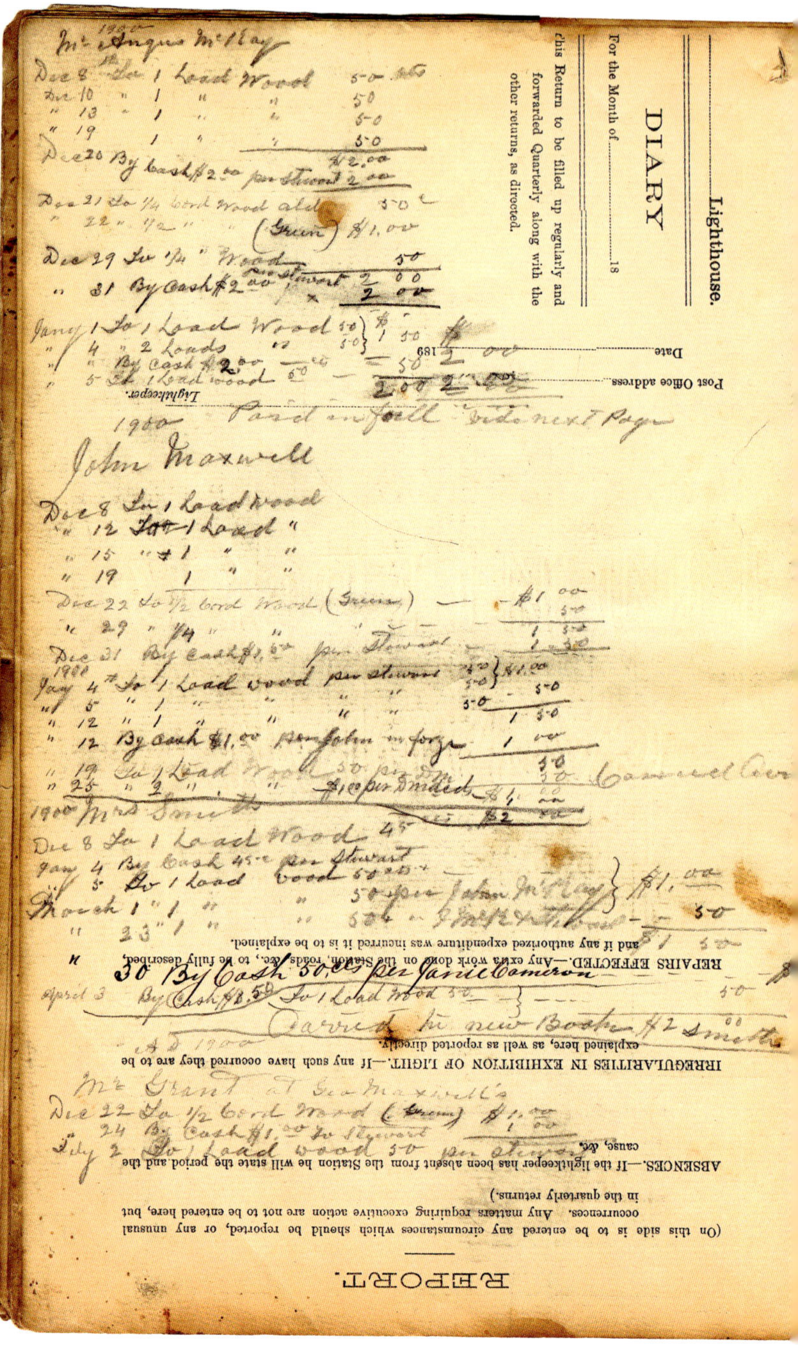

Excerpt, Diary of the Lightkeeper at Clarke's Cove, Inverness County, December 1900.
Joseph D. Matheson fonds, MG 12.178.2. Beaton Institute, Cape Breton University.

Department of Marine and Fisheries, Canada.—Lighthouse Service.

Diary of Lightkeeper at Clarke's Cove *for the month of* December 1900

Begin on Saturday 1st day

WEATHER.	WIND. A.M.	WIND. P.M.	Day of Month.	TIME OF LIGHTING.		TIME OF EXTINGUISHING.		TIME OF BURNING.		OIL USED. Galls	OIL USED. Pts.	Chimneys.	Wicks.	REMARKS.
S Shine	N W	N W	1	4	15	7	15							
"	" "	" "	2	4	15	7	15							
"	N	N	3	4	15	7	15							
Overcast	N	"	4	4	20	7	15							
Storm (Heavy)	N E	N E	5	4	20	7	20							Heavy Snow Storm all day
"	N	N	6	4	20	7	20							
[illegible]cast	S W	S W	7	4	20	7	20							
[illegible]in	N W	N W	8	4	20	7	20							
"	S	S	9	4	20	7	20							Good Sleighing
[illegible]ld, Day,	N W	N W	10	4	25	7	20							Heavy Vapor of Sea
[illegible]ty "	" "	" "	11	4	25	7	20							" " "
[illegible]ld —	" "	" "	12	4	25	7	25							
[illegible]in A.M. Snow P.M.	E	S	13	4	25	7	25	Barge Grandee, Tow Boat D L Thomas						
	N	N	14	4	25	7	25							
	N	N	15	4	25	7	25							
Gloomy	"	"	16	4	25	7	30							
"	"	"	17	4	25	7	30							
	"	"	18	4	25	7	30							
	W	W	19	4	25	7	30	Barge Grandee & D Thomas, left						
	"	"	20	4	25	7								
	"	"	21	4	25	7	30							
	N E	N E	22	4	25	7	40							
	" "	" "	23	4	25	7	40							
[illegible]A.M. Fair P.M.	S W	S W	24	4	25	7	40							
	N W		25	4	25	7	40							
	" "		26	4	25	7	40							
	" "		27	4	25	7	40							
	" "		28	4	25	7	40	Robt H McInnes Died						
	S W	S W	29	4	25	7	40	John W McLean Killed						
	W	W	30	4	25	[illegible]	40							
	E N E	N E	31	4	25	[illegible]	30	funerals today						Malagash

In exhibition of light ....

In house lamps ....

At fog alarm station..........

Destroyed, spilt, &c..........

(No. of lamps in use in lighthouse lantern during month............)

Total..........

N.B.—Nothing must be charged to the lights except the articles actually used in their exhibition.

TWO-MASTED SCHOONER

Maker unknown, Nova Scotia

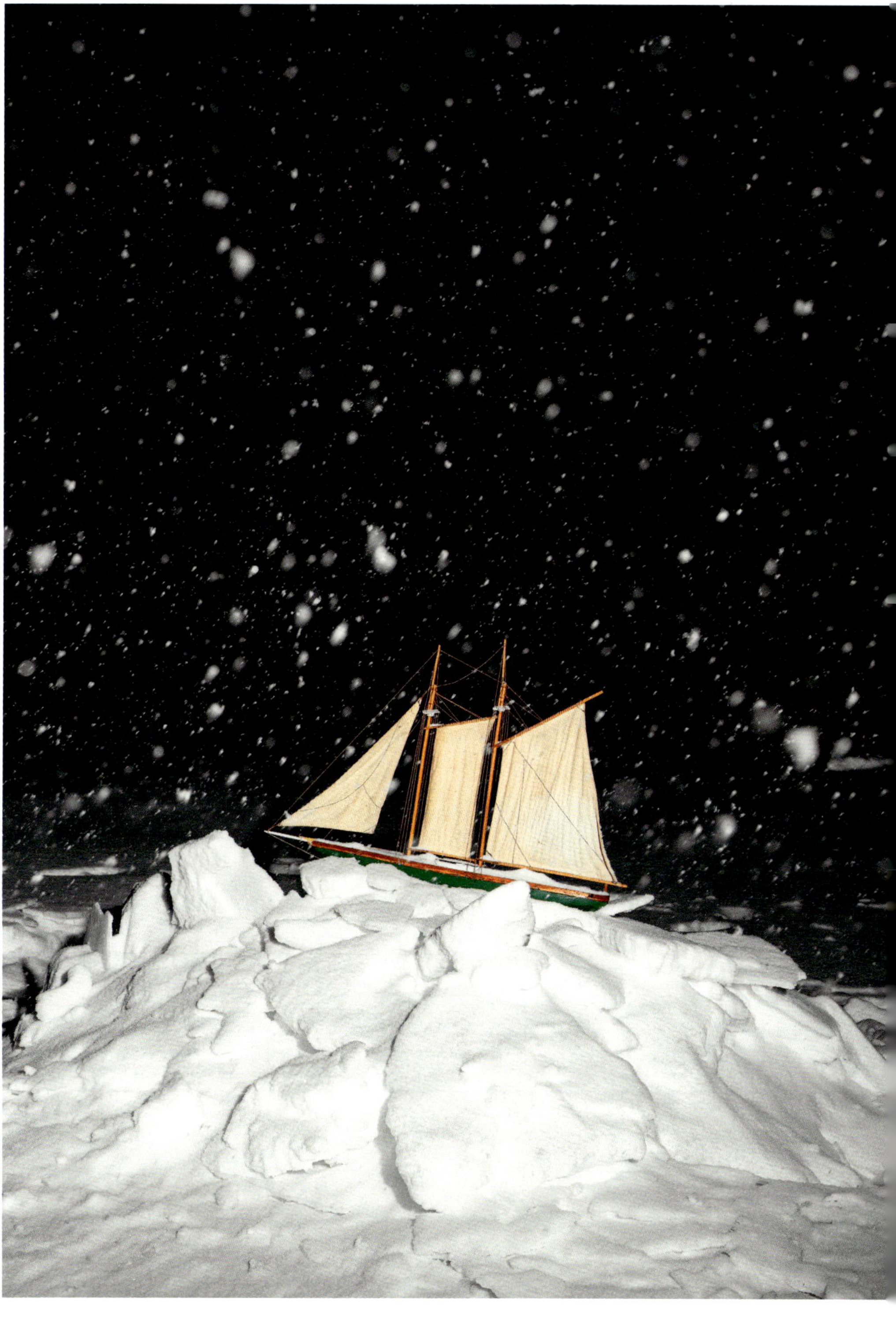

PASSENGER BOAT

Maker unknown, Newfoundland and Labrador

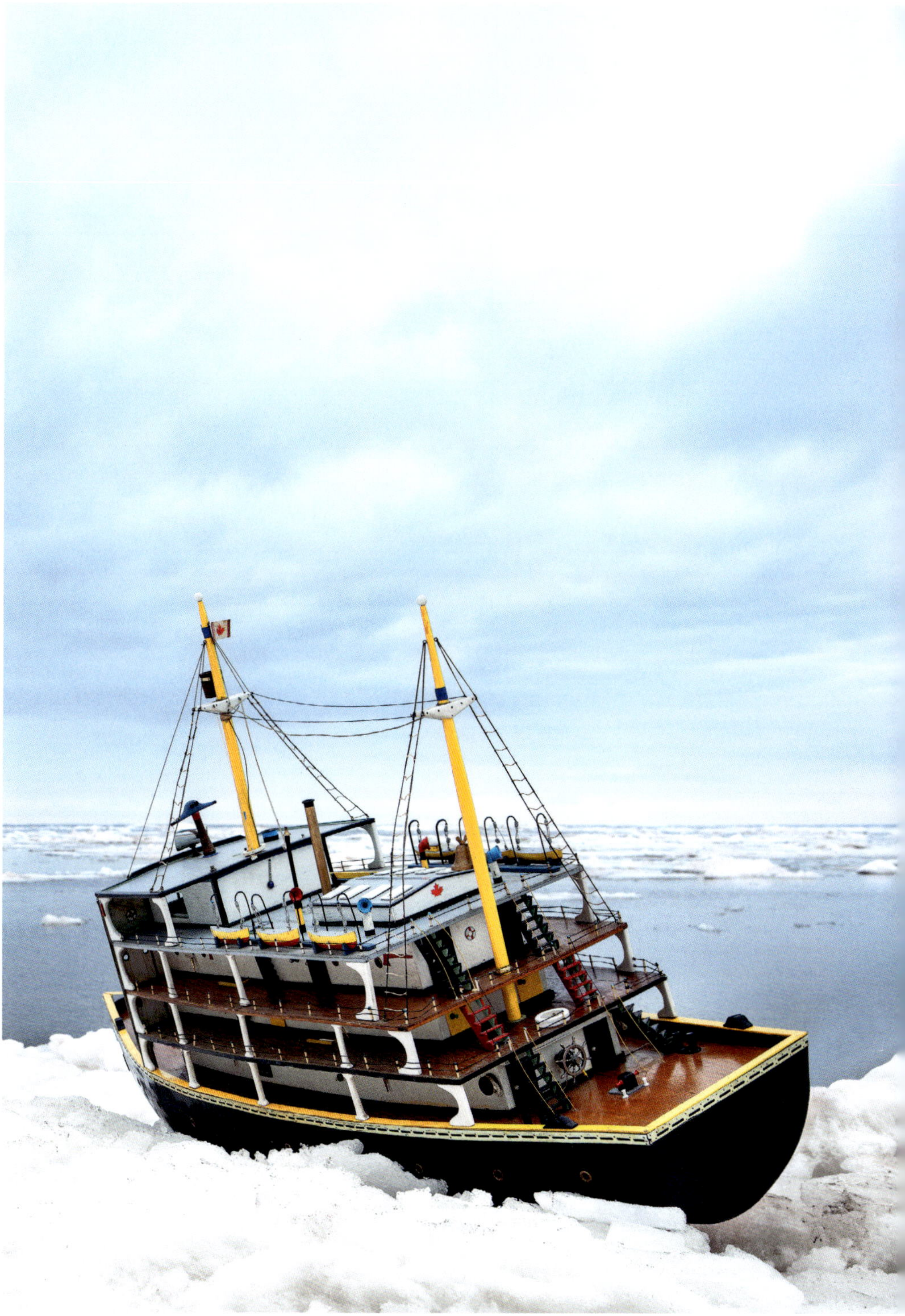

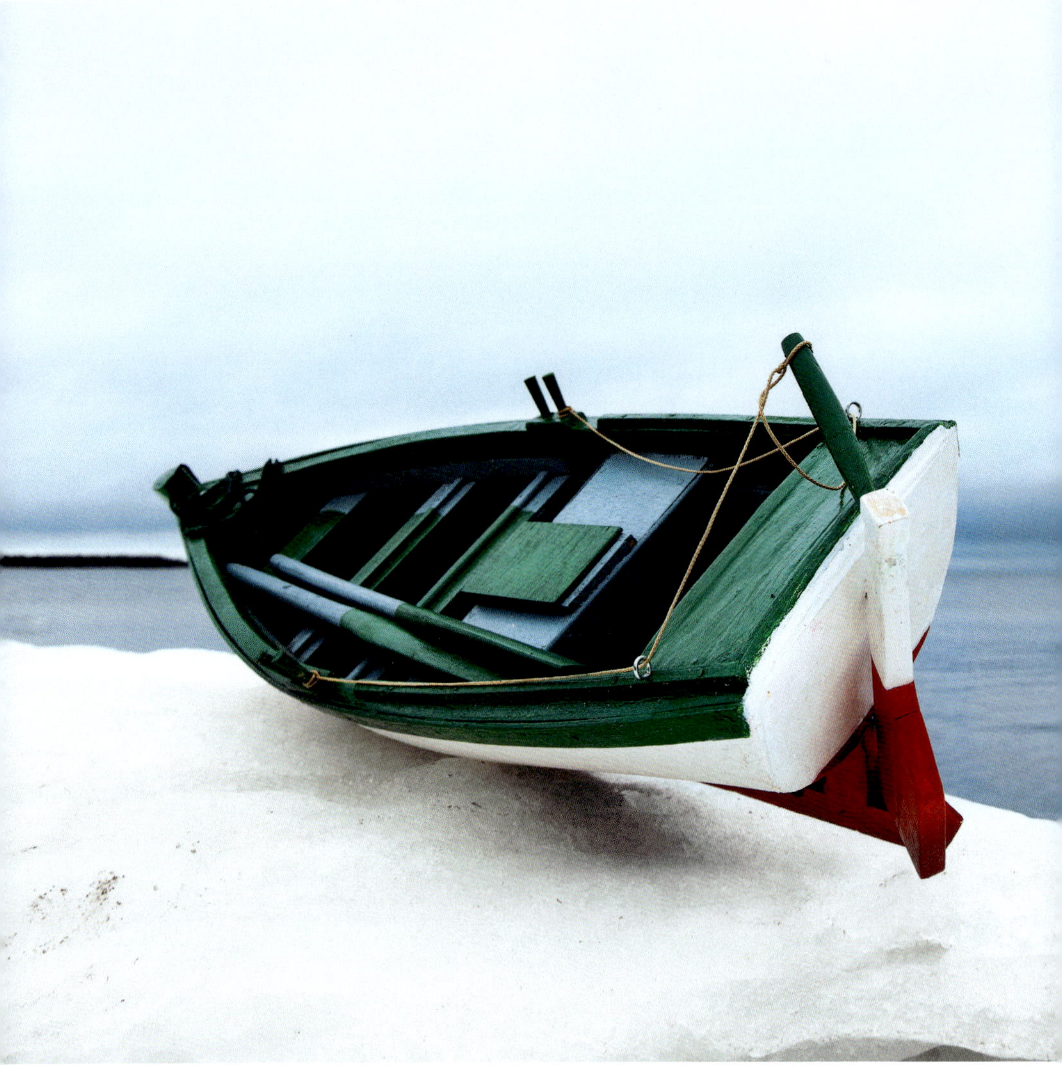

PUNT

Clayton Dominey, Burgeo, Newfoundland and Labrador

ADRIFT

PEGGY CAMERON

Biologist
Energy Producer
Writer

Irish Mountain,
Pictou County
and Halifax,
Nova Scotia

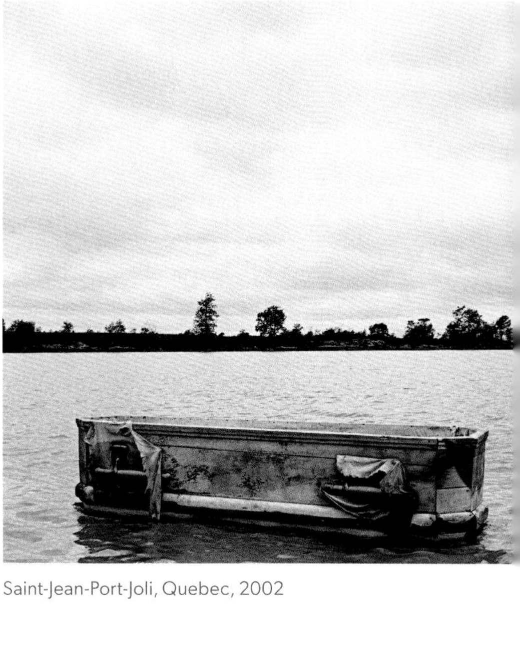

Saint-Jean-Port-Joli, Quebec, 2002

I heard this story from a woman who organized a screening of Al Gore's documentary, *An Inconvenient Truth*, in the Annapolis Valley on Valentine's Day in 2007. At that time, people were just starting to hear about climate change. There was a discussion after the film and towards the end, this older gentleman spoke in a very understated way. "Fifty years ago today I got on an ice floe and went down the shore with the tide," this man told the audience. When he got to where his sweetie lived, he got off, found her, and asked if she would marry him. She said yes. Later he got on another ice floe and went back up the shore on the return tide. This was in the Bay of Fundy. The tides are strong and the elements run from fierce to friendly. It's a very dynamic place. His conclusion was that this voyage of 50 years ago could not be done today simply because we don't have big ice floes like we did back then. He fitted his personal story into our experience of climate change.

I grew up on Irish Mountain, and we went to the beaches near Pictou Landing. In 1967, Scott Paper opened in Pictou. That summer, as kids, we watched in horror as we dipped our hands into the harbour and couldn't see them anymore. It was the effluent from the pulp mill.

I am one of the few people I know who went to a one-room school. We lived on a farm and my dad had a workhorse and sleigh. Sometimes that's how we got to school. Once, we went to school and we didn't get home for five days because there was a big snowstorm. It sounds like I might be making it up, but it's just what we did to live with the elements, not opposing the constraints of the seasons. The outdoors was a place to chase our imagination and seek whatever wild ideas we had with complete freedom. I feel like I'm an artifact from another time.

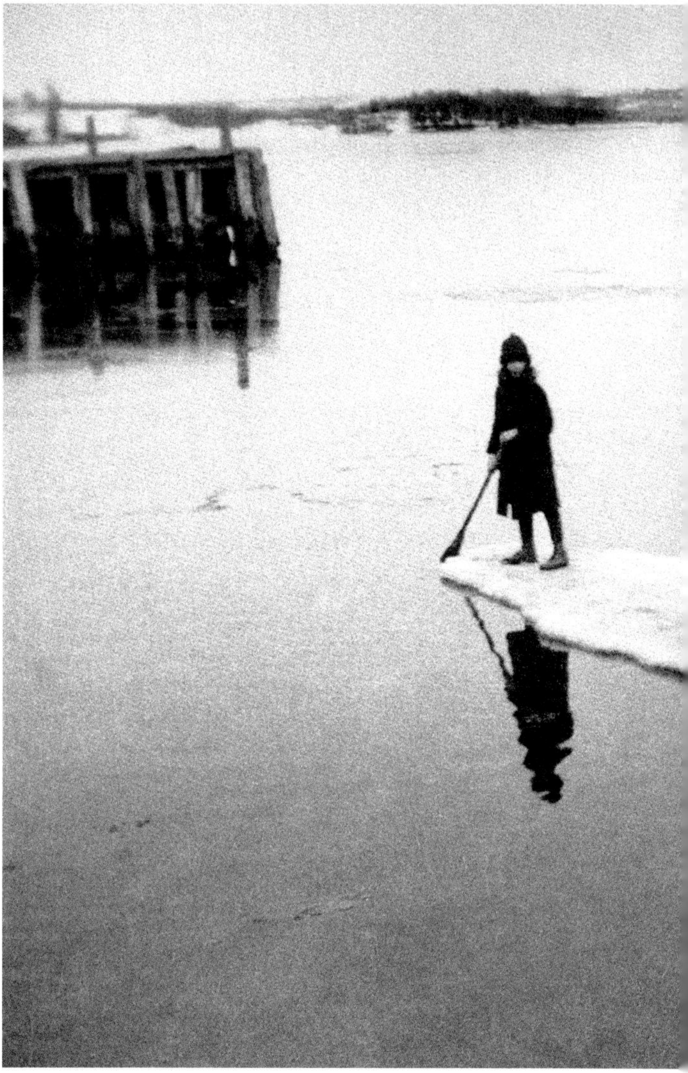

Buckley family members on a small iceberg, c. 1915–1925.
Buckley Family Nova Scotia Archives 1985-386 no. 856

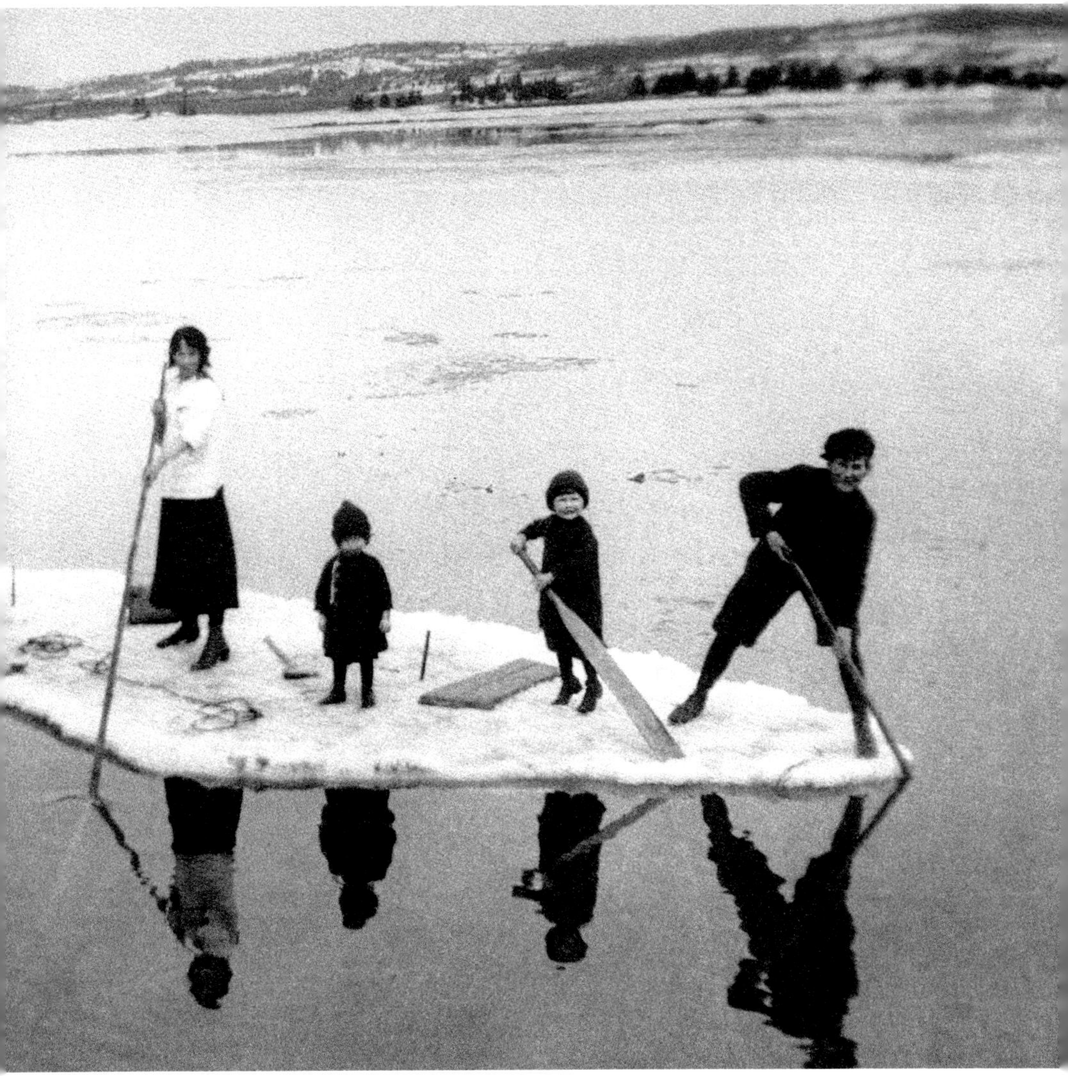

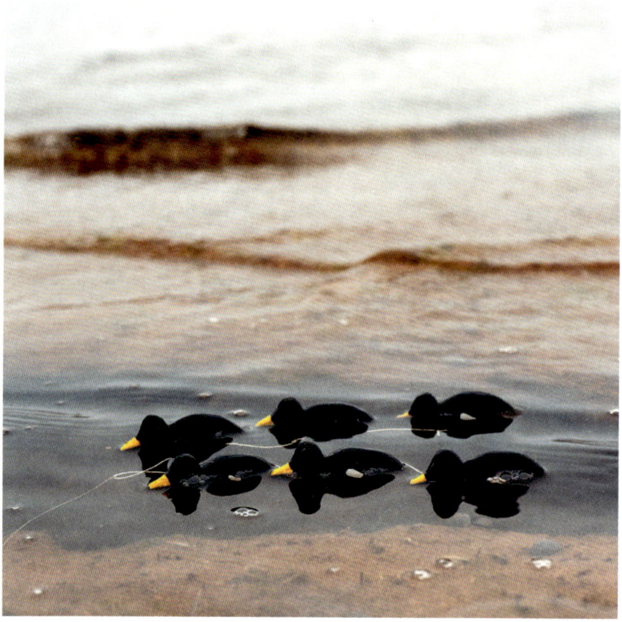

JON BOAT

Adam Ehler, New Glasgow, Nova Scotia

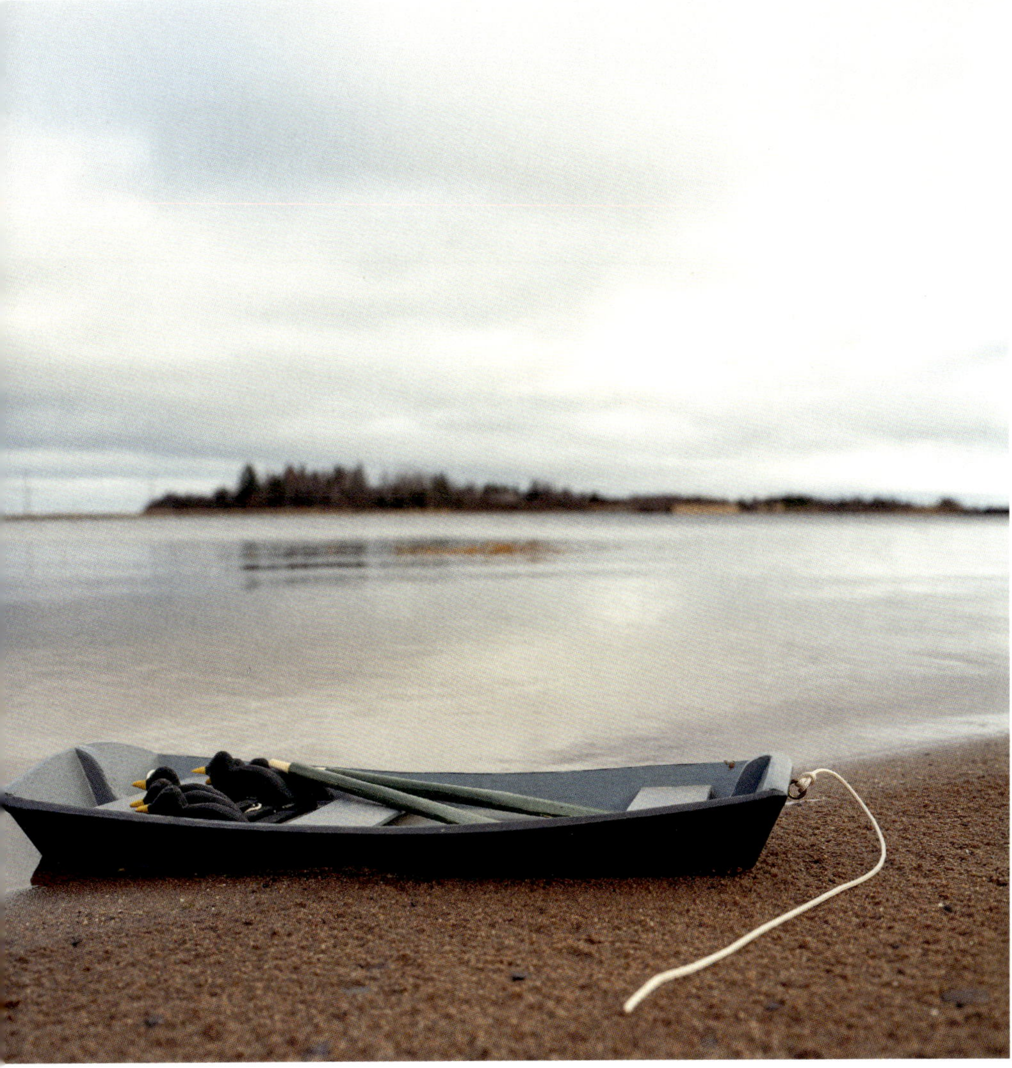

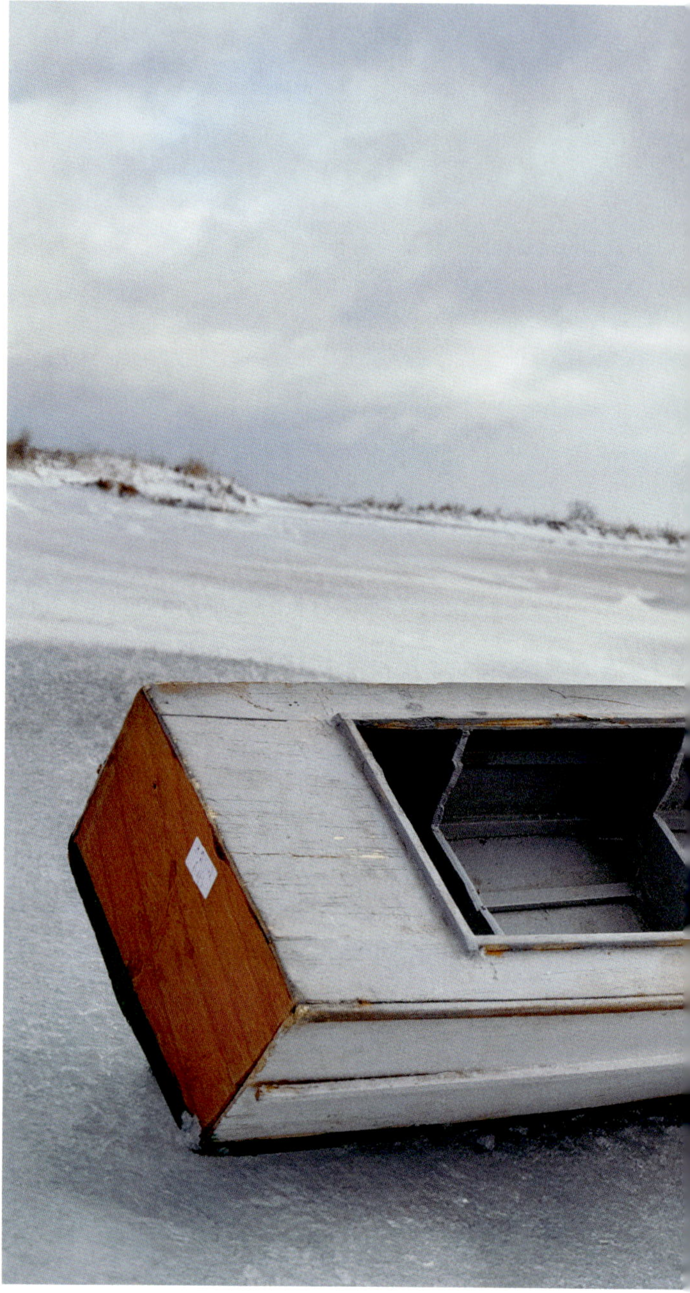

LOBSTER BOAT

Maker unknown, Nova Scotia

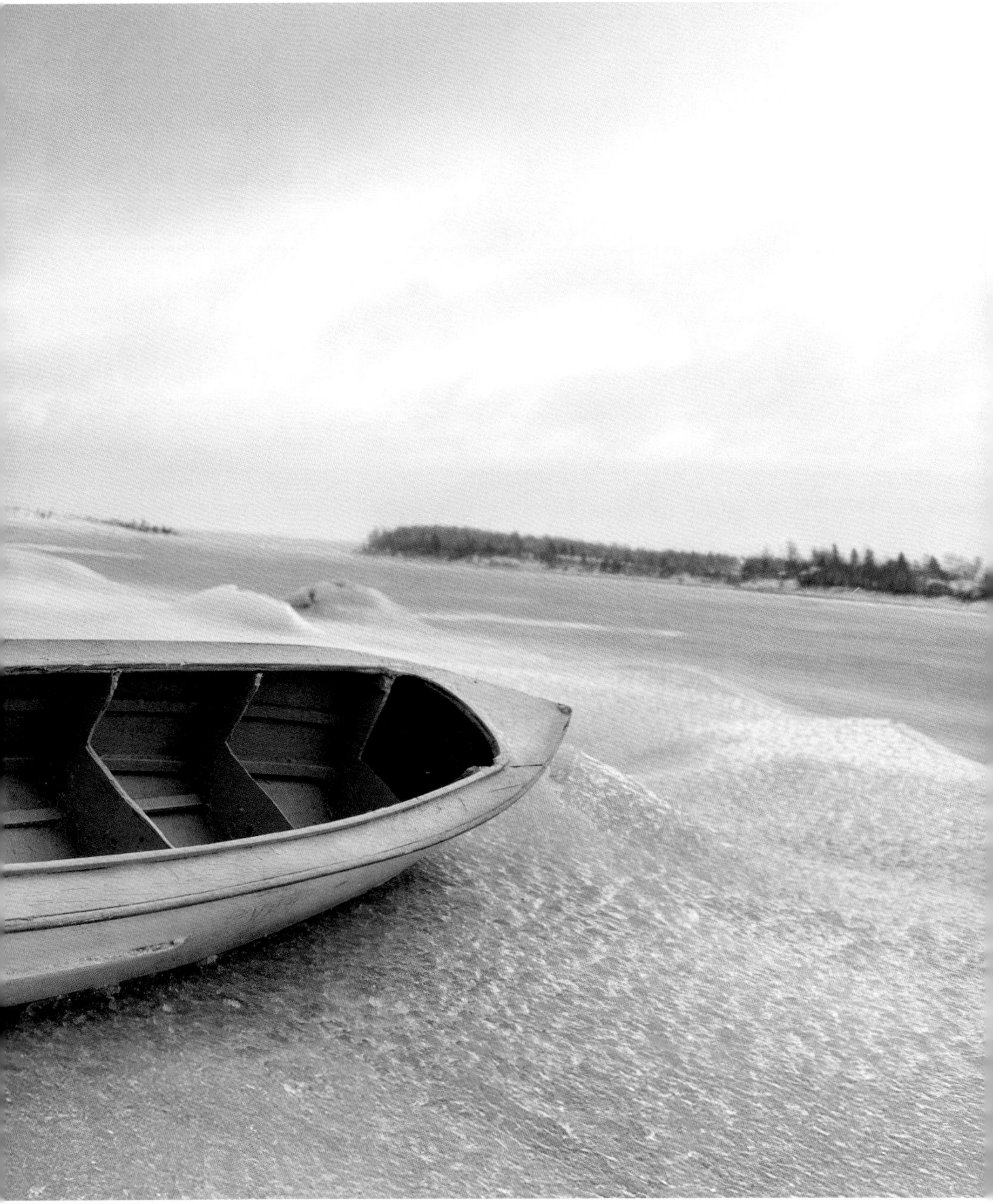

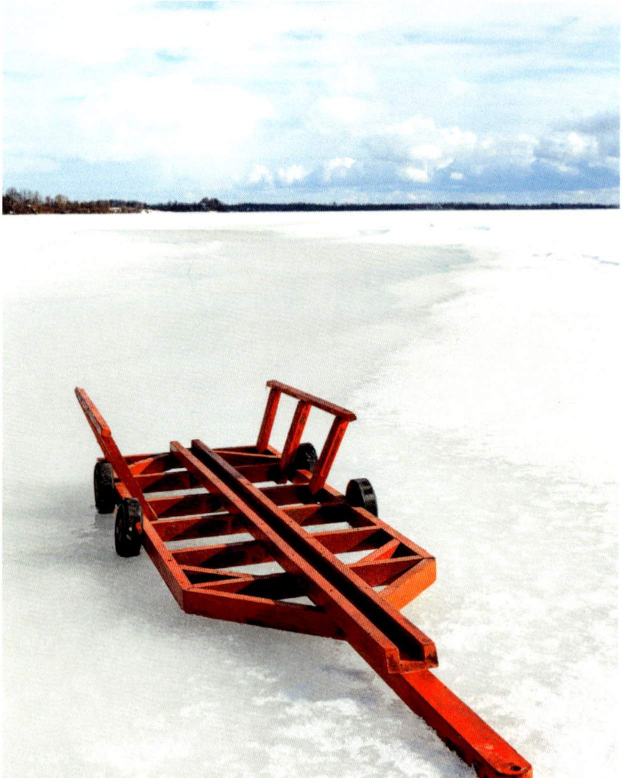

TRAILER & INSHORE SKIFF

Maker unknown, Prince Edward Island

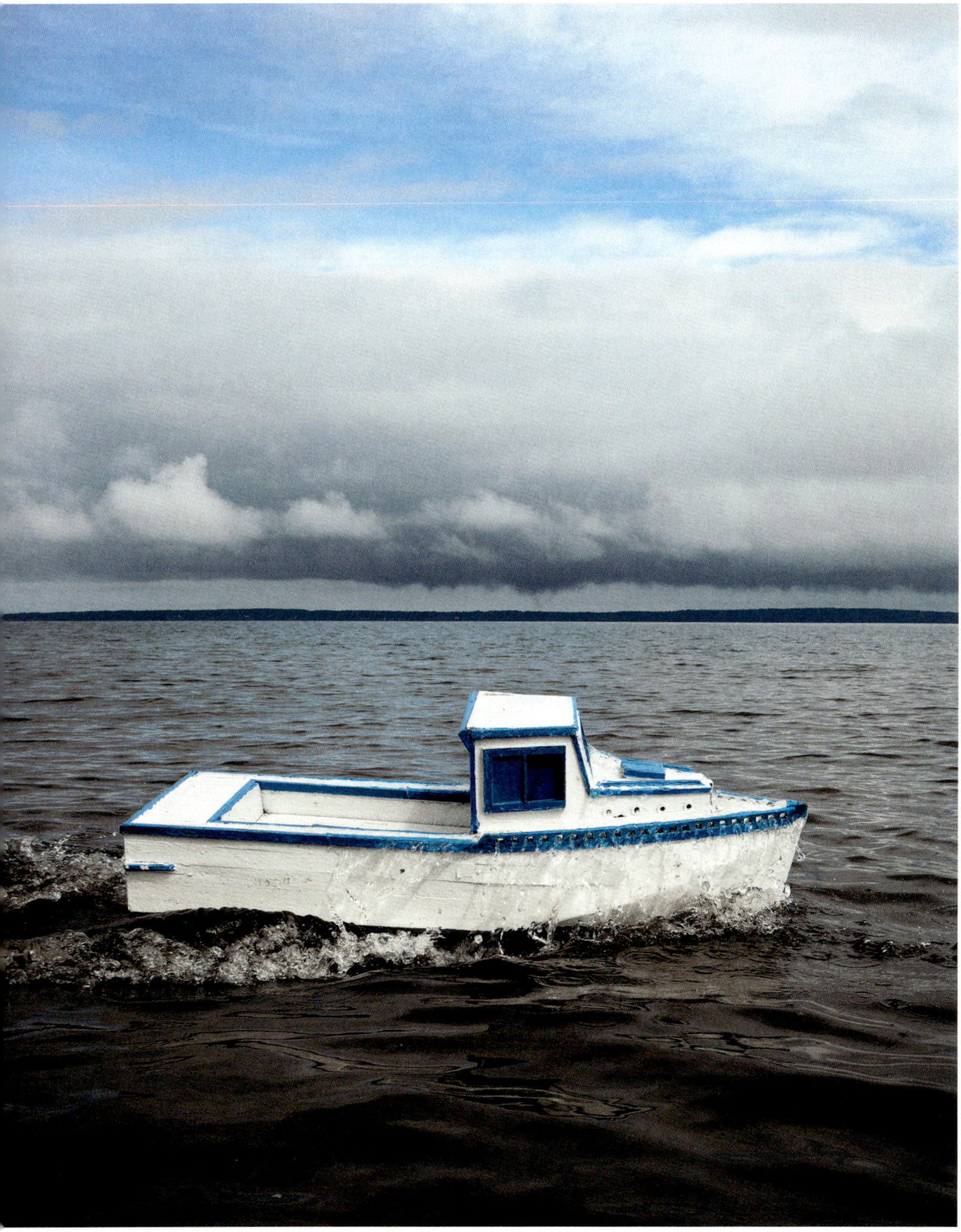

TIME WAS NEVER EMPTY

PEGGY GALE
Writer
Curator

Toronto,
Ontario

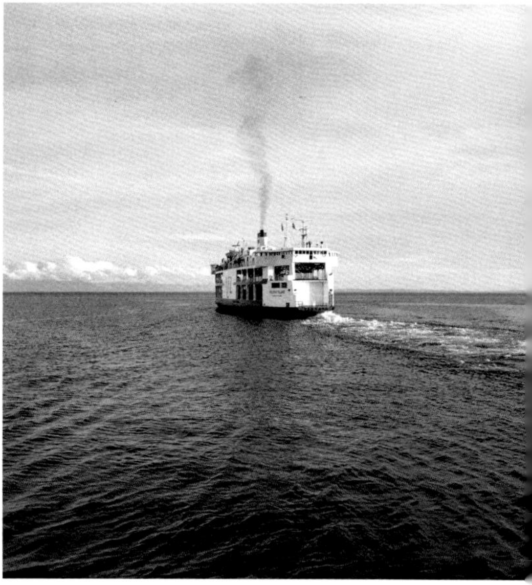

Caribou Harbour, Nova Scotia, 2002

Up along the shore ...
past Cape Anguille,
heading for Low Brook and the cliffs near Cape John

This is my past now, but still always present.

The cabin windows face due north but the eye travels from northeastern sunrise to a final northwest. Gazing from the house and field and cliff, the ocean was right there. But even the big boats looked tiny: dories and longliners and miniature ships, the Coast Guard bobbing in a friendly fashion, garbage scows or a rare cruise ship threading their way near the horizon. Sometimes a sailboat, always remarkable. Once, a famous Viking ship visited the harbour at Port aux Basques, so slim and vulnerable: hard to believe.

Where we lived, the ocean was immediate, but inaccessible. A view, at least. Local life centred on fishing, and each stream reaching the shore had at its mouth a rough camp outfitted with a couple of bunks with fishnet "mattresses," an oil-drum stove, a kettle, and some tea and sugar. Doors were unlatched; visitors might be desperate. There were stories of men found dead at cliff-tops, having managed somehow to scale the rocky wall but foundered then for sustenance, lost, hungry. One local tale tells of a group of Italians, all found dead along the cliff-tops with their empty bottles of wine.

The old days are not so far back. Even a couple of decades ago, older friends in Codroy spent the winters knitting or repairing nets, maybe building a new boat. They'd set out their gardens in the late spring—potatoes, turnip, cabbage, beets, and onions—though in early June there was often still snow in the woods. Harvest would come in August for the hay, and October for the vegetables, now big enough to last the winter. Even in the 1990s there were animals—pigs, sheep, cows, chickens—kept for the winter. Sheep led to shearing, then spinning wool, then knitting socks and finger-mitts for the "sports" who came for the fall moose hunt.

I mostly saw the weather. Fleeting sun and hazy skies, cloudy, with the clouds rarely a classic puffy white against blue. Shifting, always on the move. Over Low Brook, hidden by the folded fields, a long, narrow string of a firm white cloud—like cotton batting—traced the line of an invisible stream. Fog arrived in many forms. Sometimes gauzy, simply filling white windows. Other times, a creamy blanket on the ocean, moving towards the cliffs, then silently sliding upwards to reach the lip, maybe pausing for a moment, then slipping onto field itself, a rich, soft layer approaching the house, then the windows overtaken, white: the fog—the cloud—all around us.

Winters were long, but the time was never empty. Knitting and quilts for the women, and preserves for winter. Nets and repairs for the fishermen, and cutting and stacking wood for stoves. Whittling axe-handles, maybe. Building model boats.

A model, typically, is a miniature: created or collected lovingly, something diminutive, needing protection. A memory site, often. An embodiment: something to hold dear and with which to become one. Set on a shelf or broader surface they already float.

A model boat is not a toy, but little boats are likely a child's first attempt at carpentry—two wood sticks with a tall nail, the mast, holding them together—a step towards the big world. A private adventure.

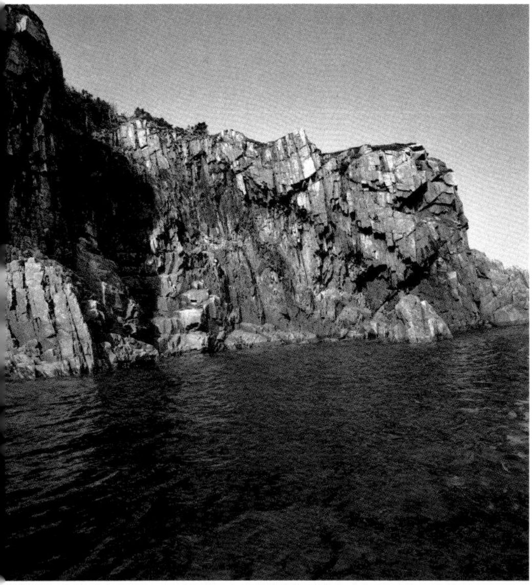

Fogo Island, Newfoundland and Labrador, 2012

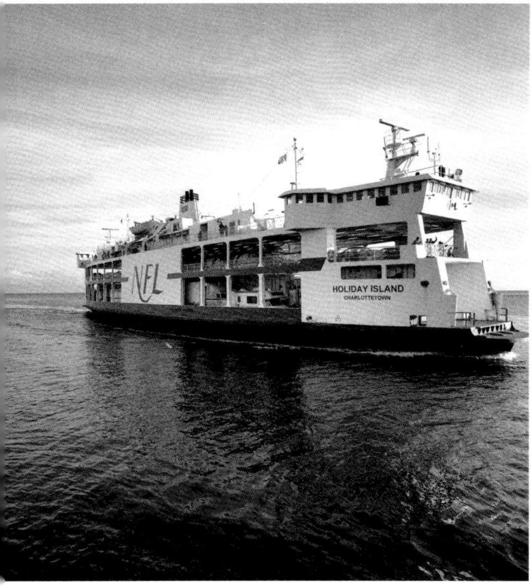

Caribou Harbour, Nova Scotia, 2002

FOLK ART BOAT

Maker unknown, Nova Scotia

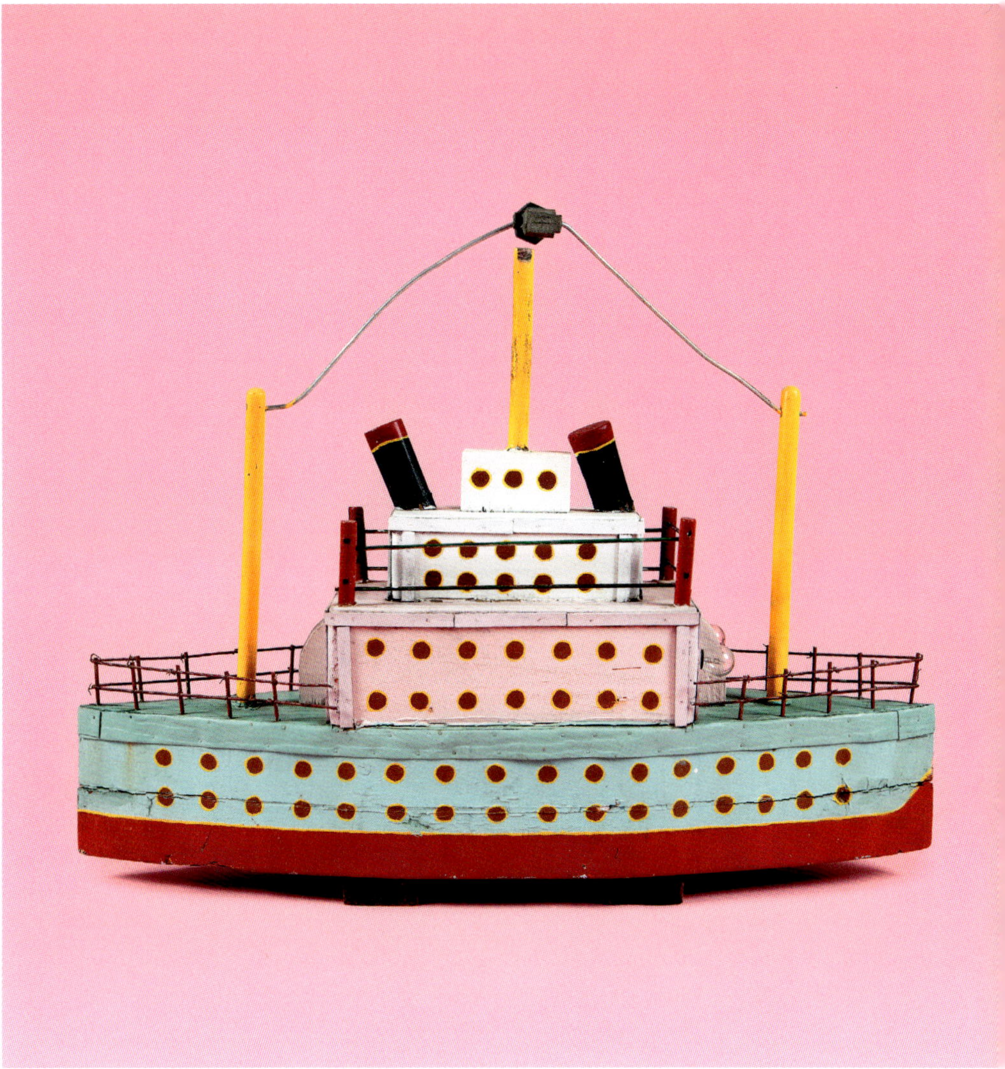

FISHING BOATS & "BLUENOSE," TWO-MASTED SCHOONER

Floyd and Randy Stewart, Lockeport, Nova Scotia

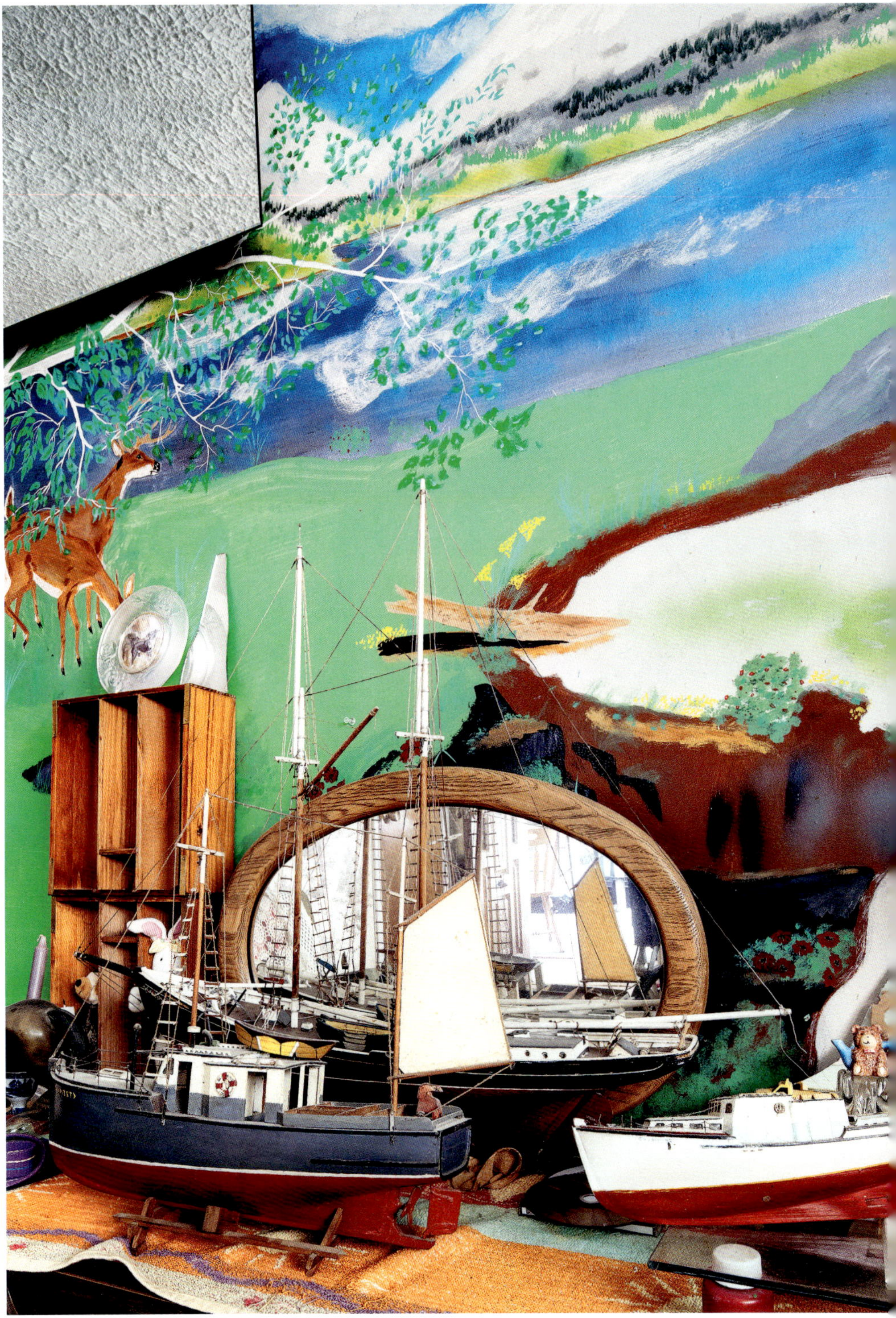

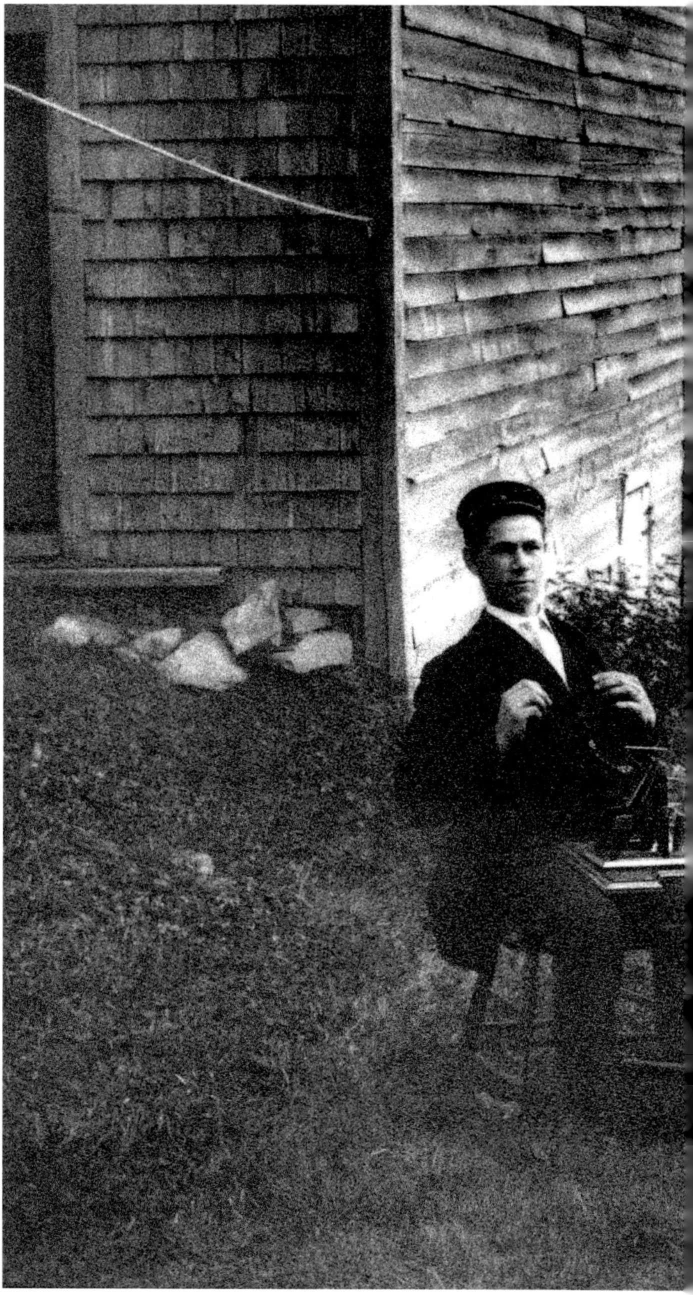

Buckley family members pose with some of their models and inventions, c. 1900; Guysborough Harbour in the background. Buckley Family Nova Scotia Archives 1985-386 no. 53 / negative: N-7251

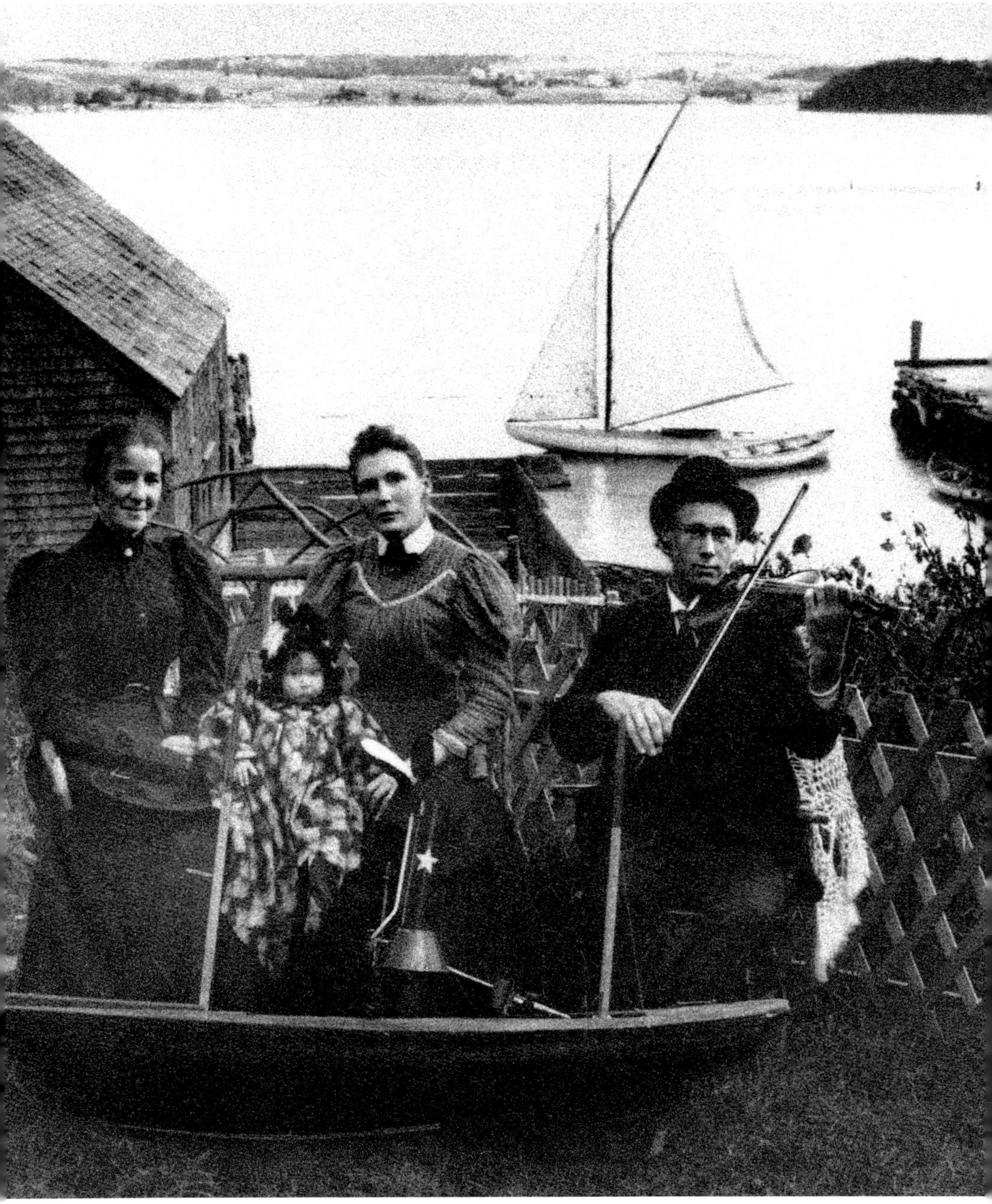

THREE-MASTED SCHOONER

Maker unknown, Nova Scotia

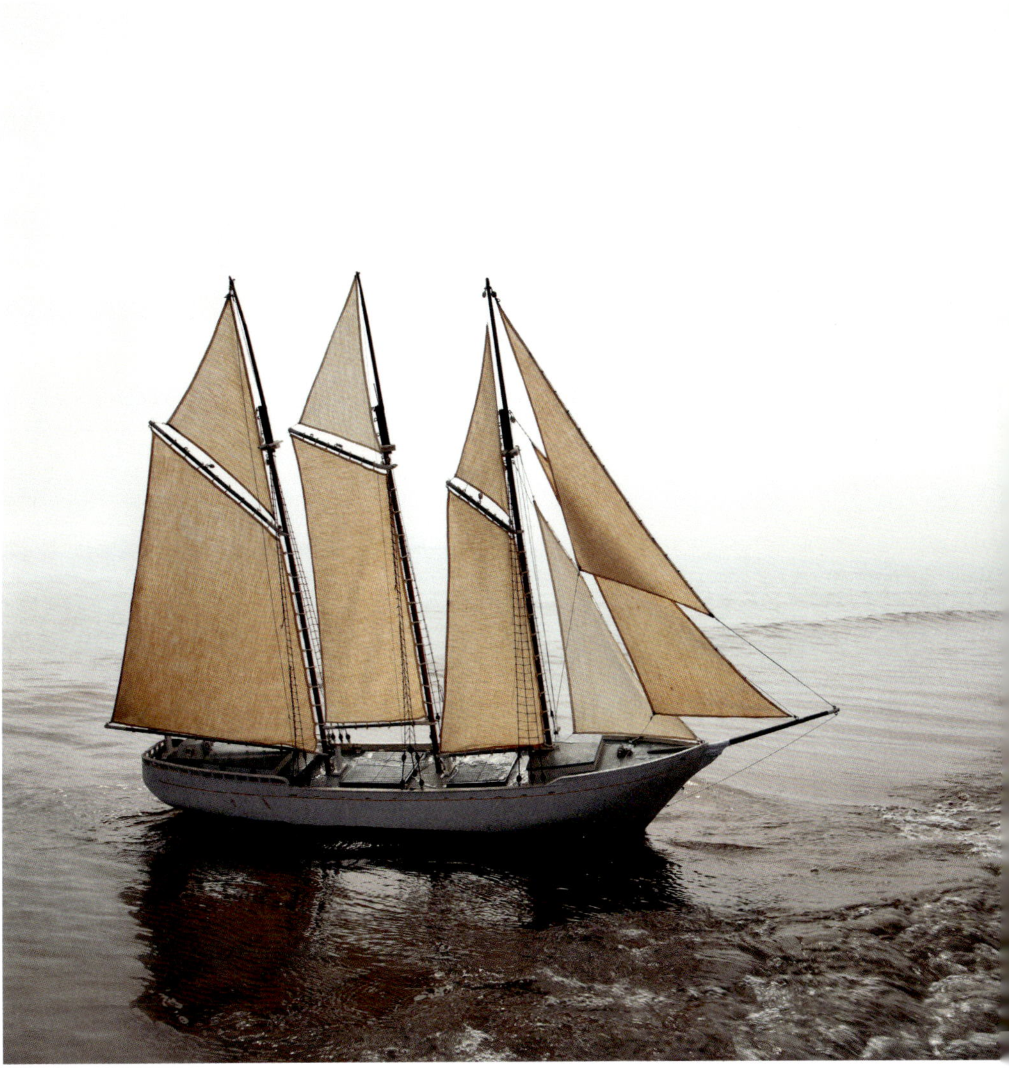

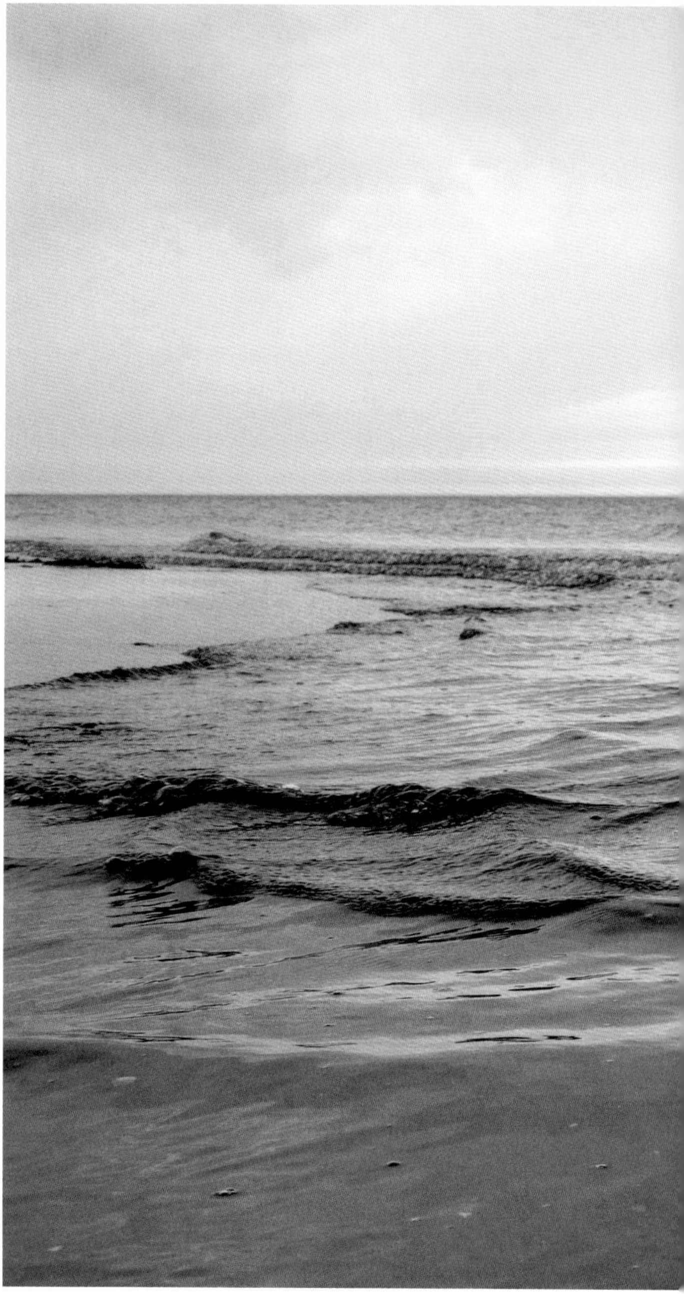

BARQUE

Maker unknown, Nova Scotia

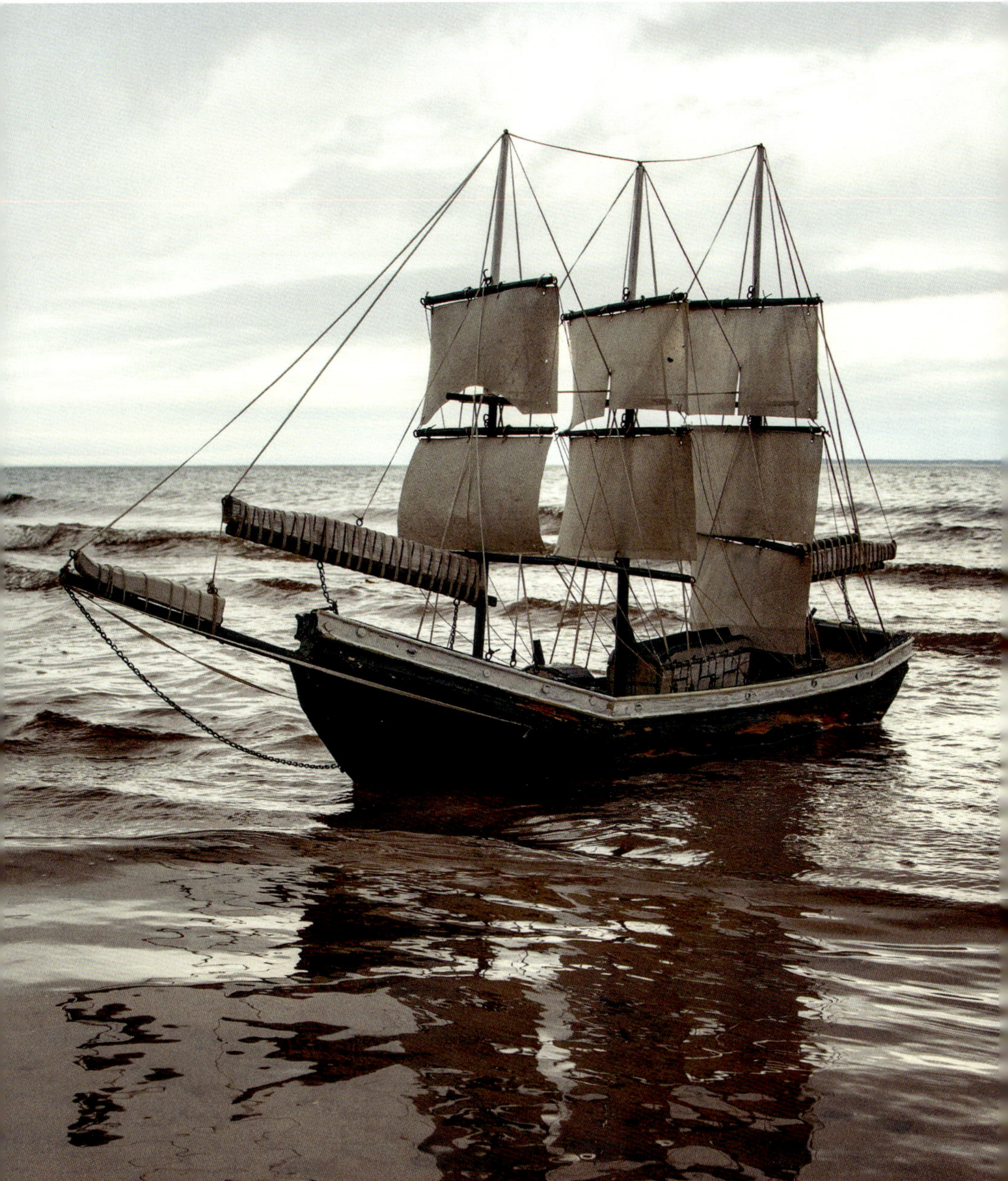

GIFTED TO OTHERS

JIM TURPLE
Model Maker

Hardwood Hill,
Nova Scotia

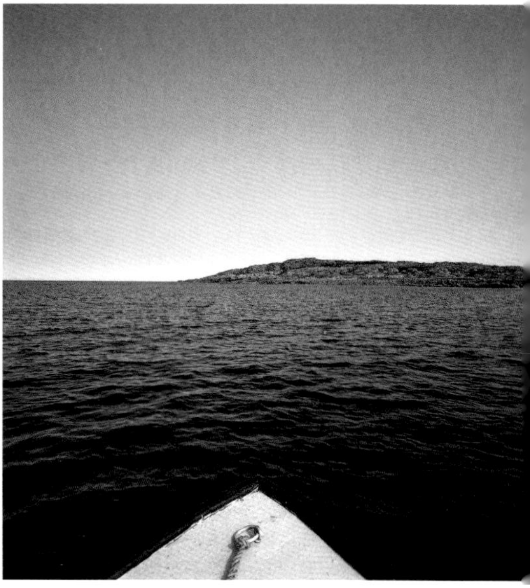

Fogo Island, Newfoundland and Labrador, 2012

What makes a model successful to me? If it looks decent and floats for kids to play with then it is successful. I grew up with designs from my dad's boats. I am proud of my models because they resembled in some way the boats that Dad built. I have probably built at least 30 or more models and most of them I give away.

My dad and mum married in 1940 and I was born in 1951. Dad purchased the Pictou Island farm from his father. I lived on Pictou Island until September 1964. My dad was a master boat builder. He built over 22 wooden lobster boats. In 1940, he built the iceboat islanders used for winter travelling to the mainland.

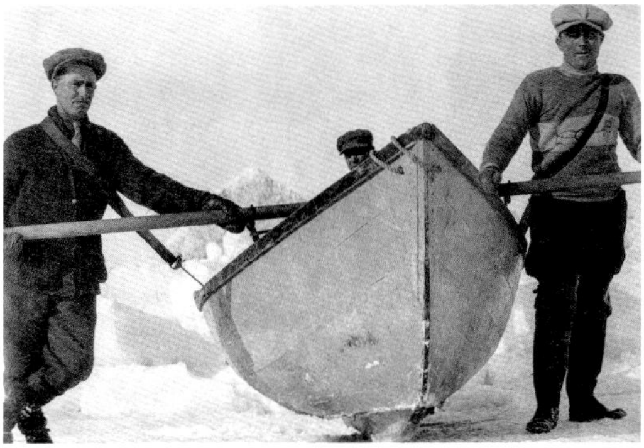

Iceboat of Pictou Island, 1940 by Vincent Turple. Photograph Northumberland Fisheries Museum, Pictou, Nova Scotia

In 1980, the Northumberland Fisheries Museum asked me if I would make a model for them. I had already given the museum the "Lucky Lady," which was a round-bottom model boat. My dad and I used to race his lobster boats against PEI fishermen, who mainly had V-bottom boats, which were very fast. So, I figured that I would make a V-bottom. I put that model together in the basement of my home here on Hardwood Hill Road during the winter months. Everything would be measured as per what I considered it to be. I never drew a model out prior to building it. It was my own design and not based exactly on any real boat. That's "Wild Thing."

"WILD THING," LOBSTER BOAT

Jim Turple, Hardwood Hills, Nova Scotia

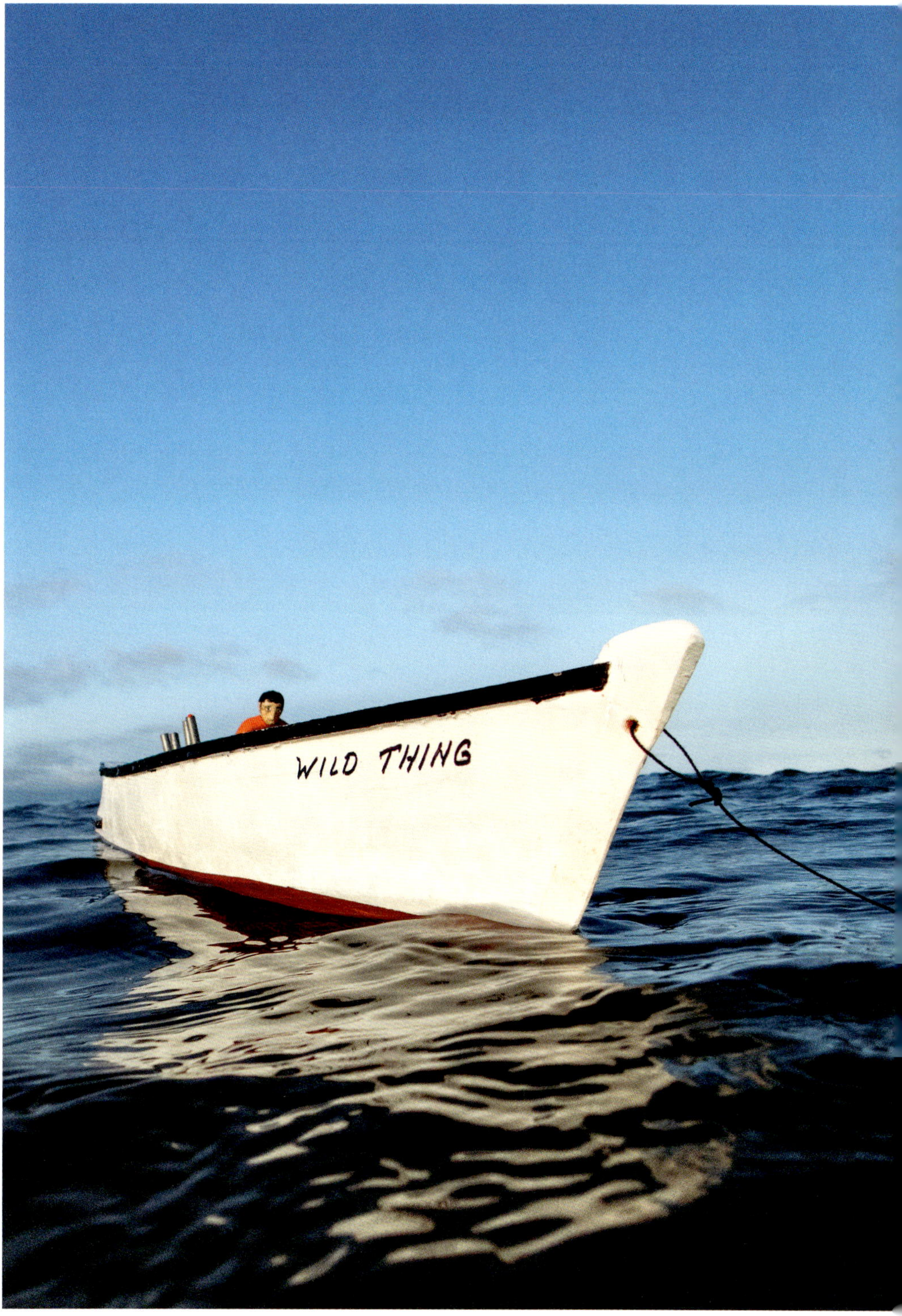
WILD THING

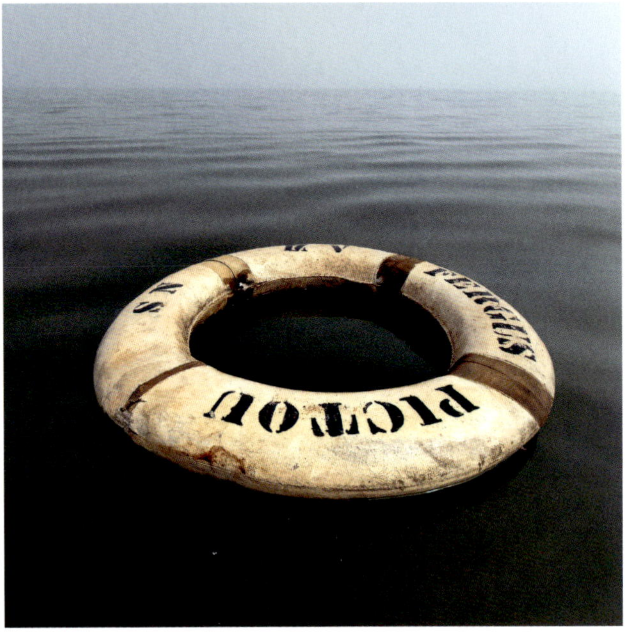

LIFEBUOY

Pictou, Nova Scotia

"WILD THING," LOBSTER BOAT

Jim Turple, Hardwood Hills, Nova Scotia

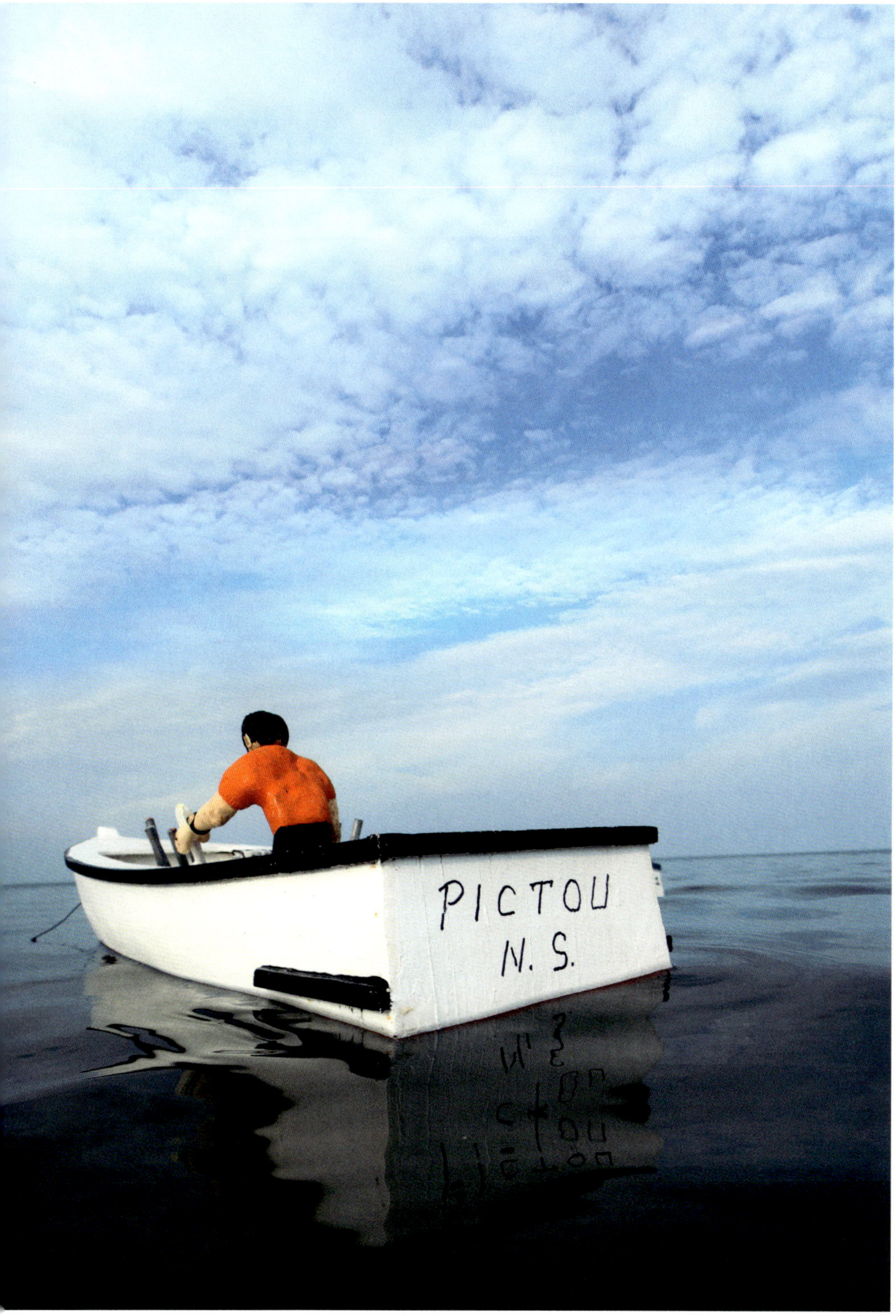
PICTOU
N. S.

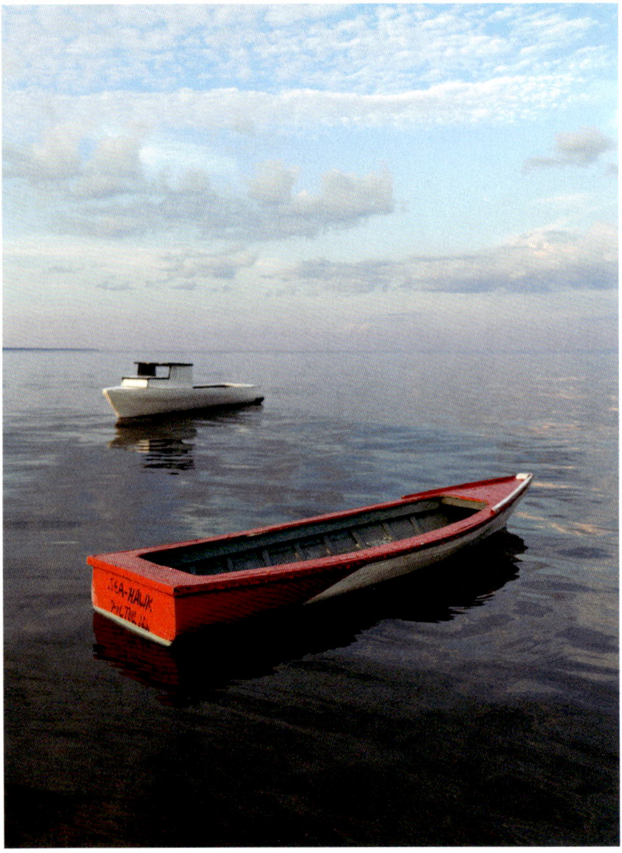

"SEA HAWK" & "WHITE LIGHTNING," LOBSTER BOATS

Jim Turple, Hardwood Hill, Nova Scotia

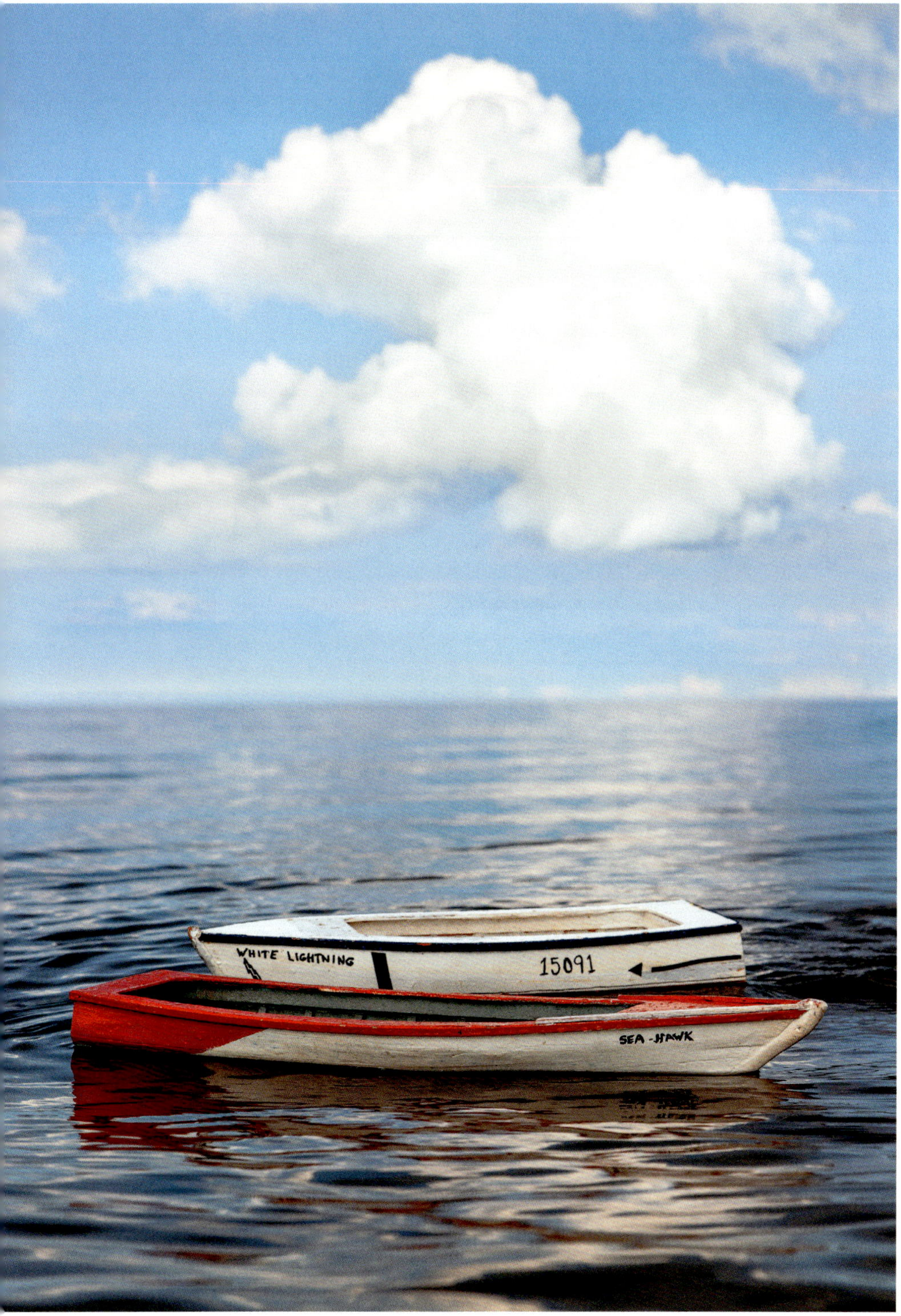
WHITE LIGHTNING
15091
SEA-HAWK

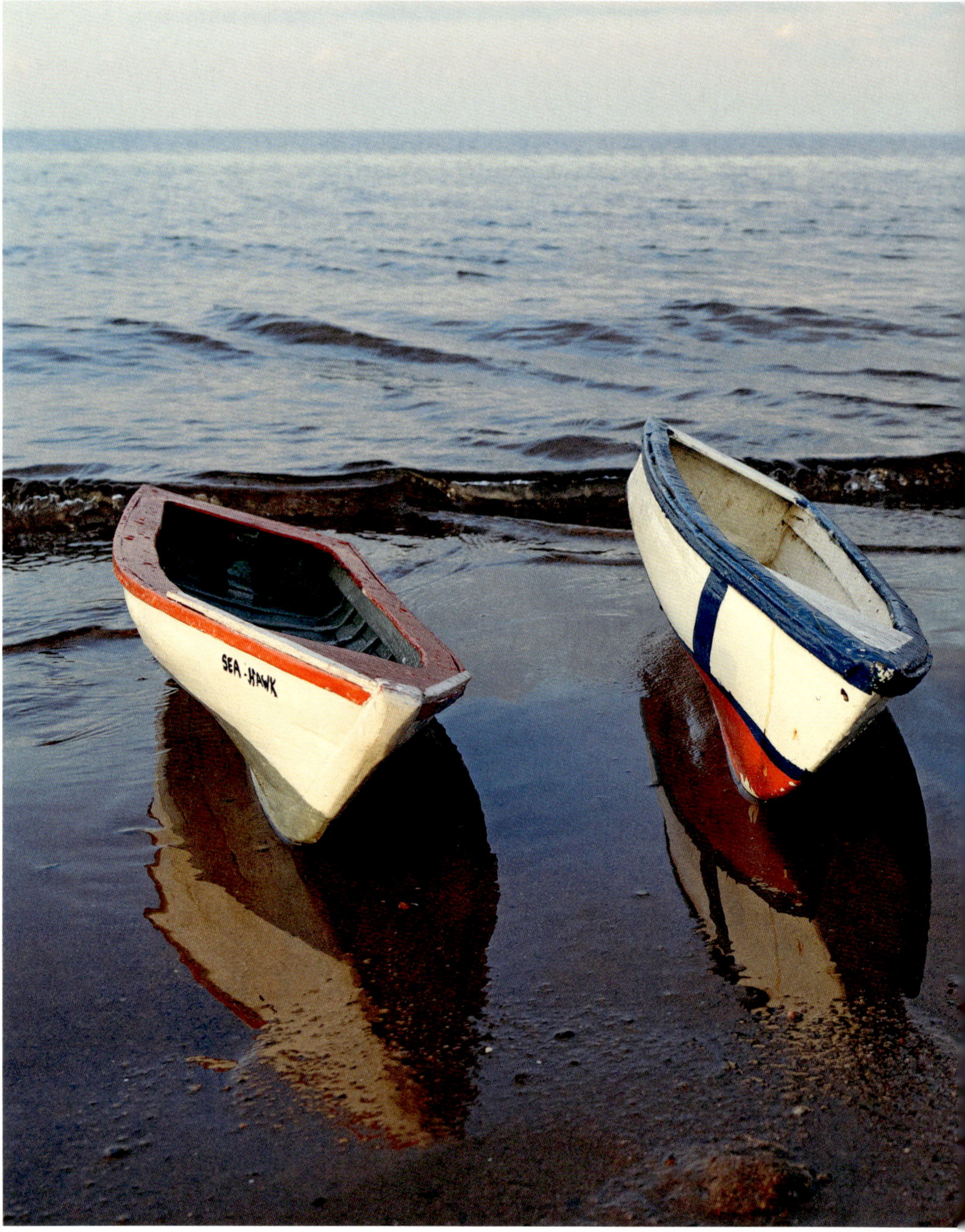

"SEA HAWK," "WHITE LIGHTNING," LOBSTER BOATS

Jim Turple, Hardwood Hill, Nova Scotia

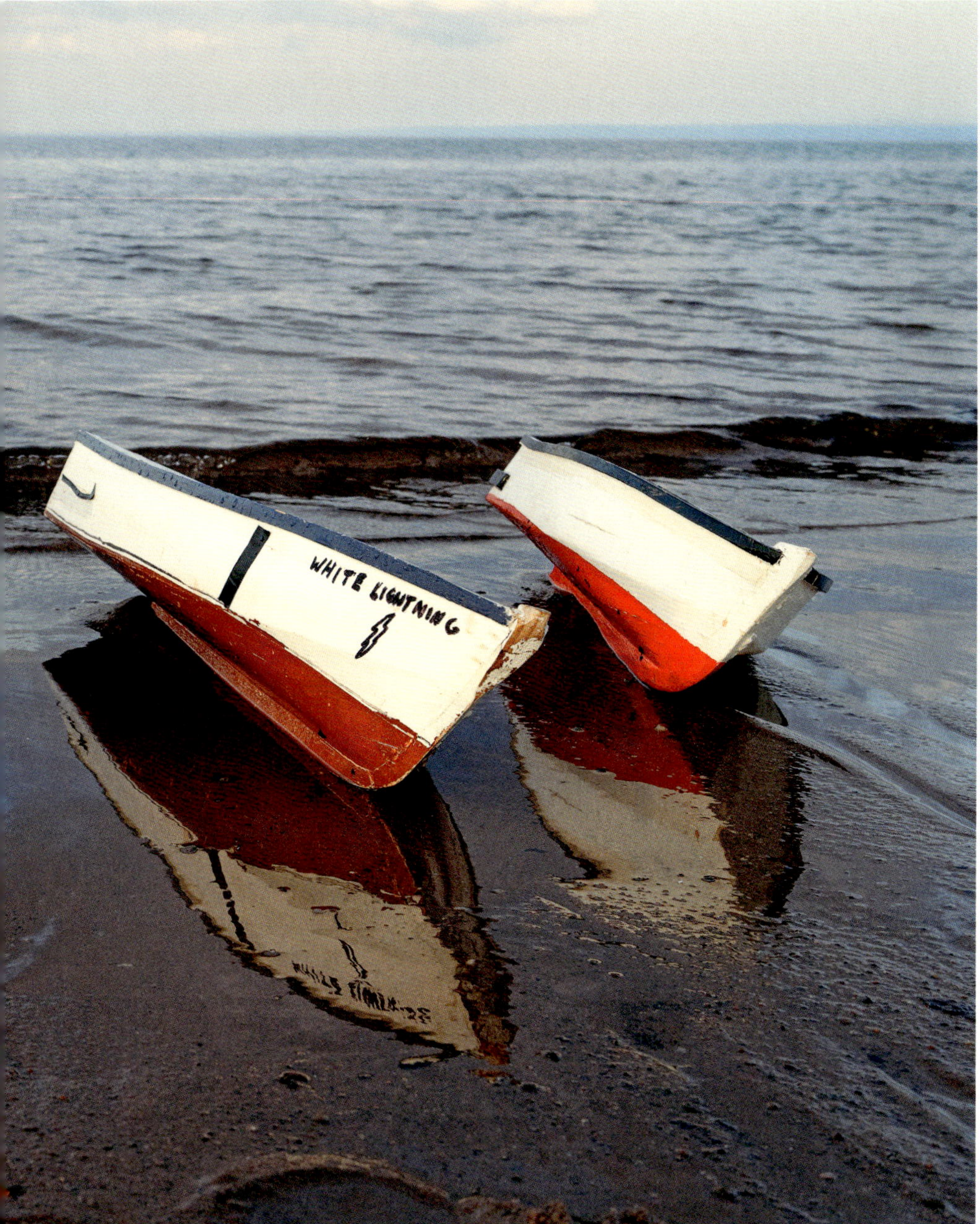
WHITE LIGHTNING

TEACHING AND TESTING

JOHN RAE

Marine Educator

Entrepreneur

Halifax,
Nova Scotia

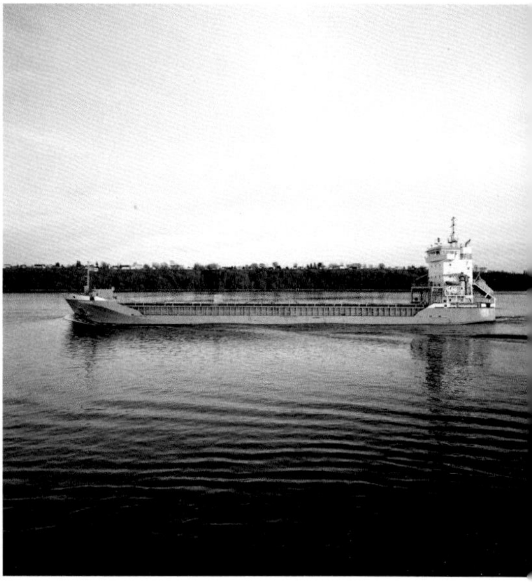

Gulf of St. Lawrence, 2002

My father founded Captain Andrew J. Rae and Sons Ltd. in 1965, and one of the things we did is build model boats for marine education. We built a stability model for the Pictou Fisheries School in 1968 or 1969. National Sea Products lent us the lines and plans of their newest trawler, the "Cape Argos," and we followed those specifications. At that time fishing vessels were getting bigger, going further out to sea, and Transport Canada was bringing in regulations. Crews needed certification.

When a vessel is designed, the naval architect calculates a "point of no return" for the ship's centre of gravity. If you load a vessel so that the centre of gravity goes above this point, known as the metacentre, the vessel will capsize. The science of ship stability involves balancing the variable weights of fuel, stores, and cargo with the real-life sea conditions, according to the ship's shape and draft.

The Pictou model is built of fiberglass and sits in a tank of water. It has fuel and water tanks that you can fill or drain; weights that simulate packing ice, trawl nets, and fish catches; and another weight you can move up and down to change the centre of gravity. You could see, in layman's terms, how tippy or non-tippy the boat was in different conditions—for instance, if ice gets on the superstructure. An inch of ice might weigh, I don't know, 10 tons; two inches of ice, 20 tons. In that case, rather than plowing the vessel into the sea and ending up with layers of frozen spray, you may reduce your speed and kind of ride things out a bit so that you don't put yourself in a dangerous situation. Like that saying, *it's better felt than telt*.

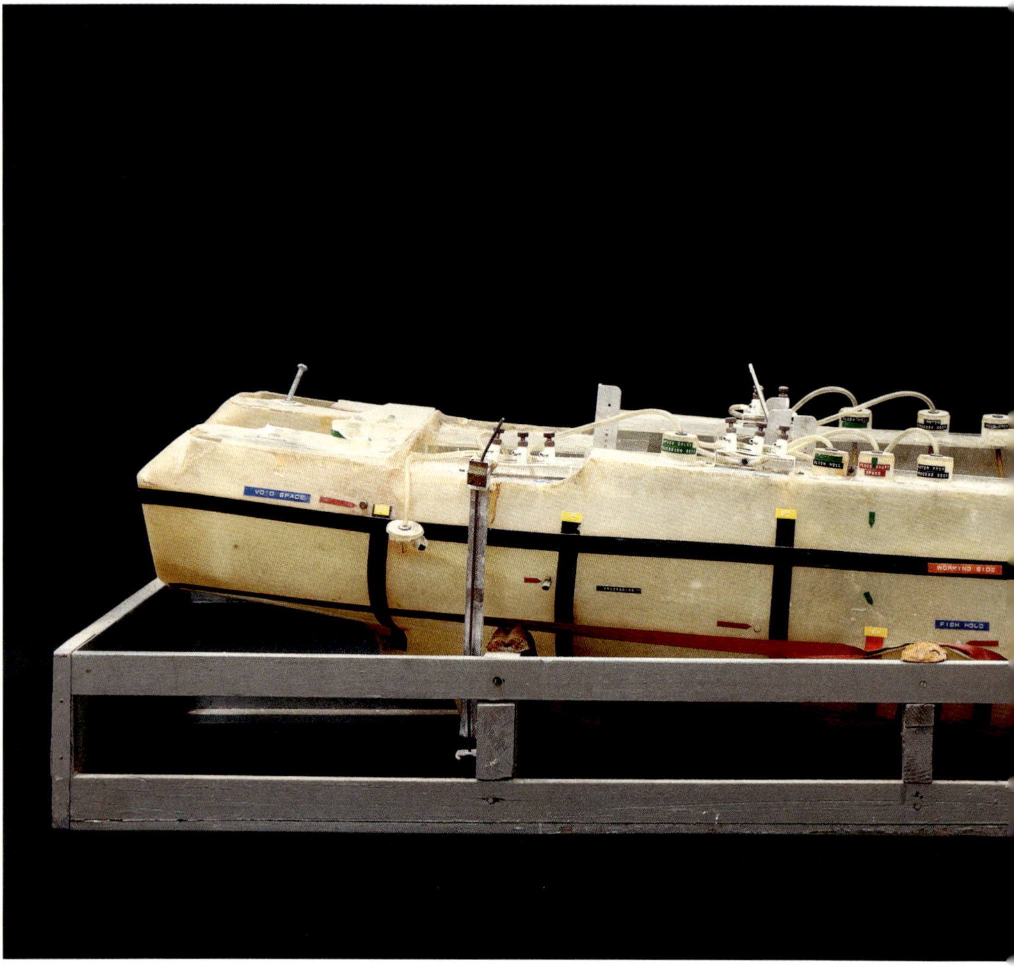

STABILITY MODEL

Captain Andrew J. Rae and Sons Ltd., Halifax, Nova Scotia

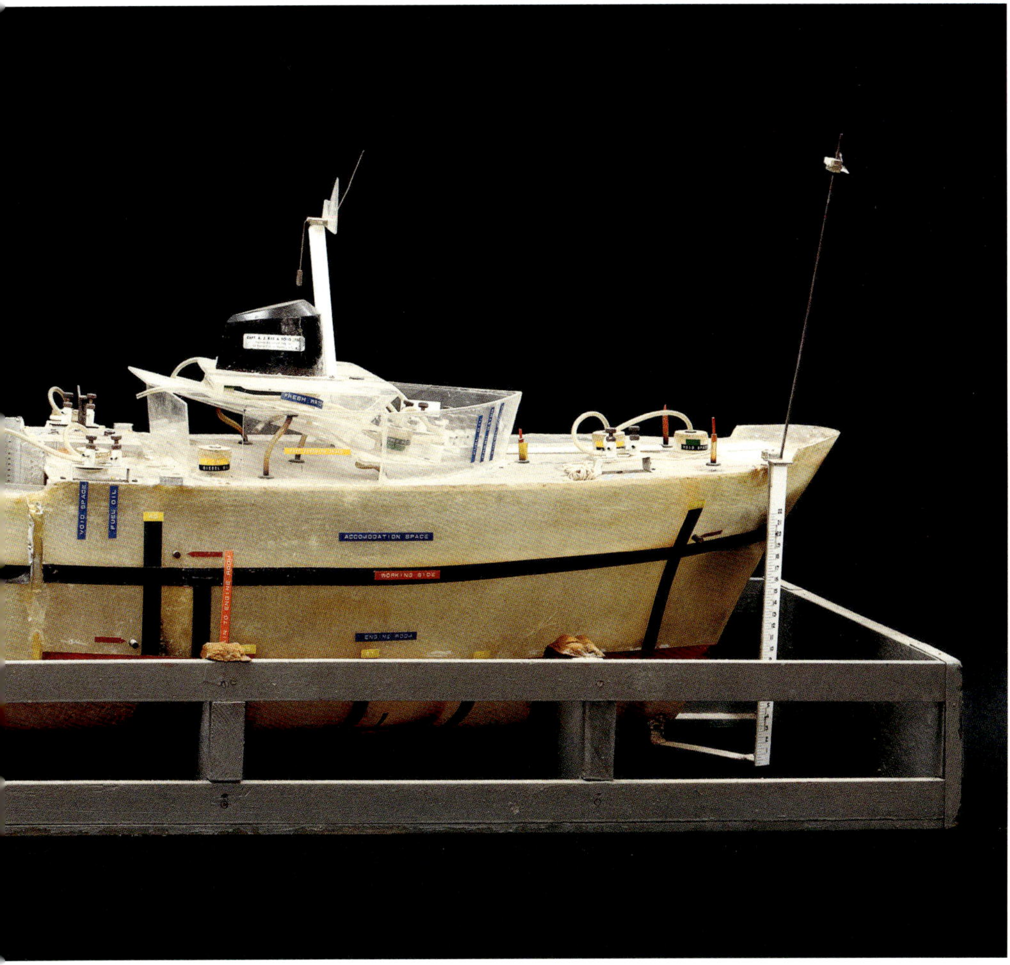
VOID SPACE
FUEL OIL
DIESEL OIL
ACCOMODATION SPACE
WORKING SIDE
ENGINE ROOM

WILLIAM KNIGHT
Curator
Historian

Ottawa,
Ontario

Some model boats have had working lives as research instruments. Mounted in wind tunnels or dragged through towing tanks, their simplified forms measure wind and water resistance.

Outside of these contexts, such models appear unfinished, half-thought. Three National Research Council wind-tunnel models, made in the 1960s and '70s, are even sinister, with dark stealthy hulls outlined in high contrast white pin-striping.

One of them, the destroyer escort model, reflects Cold War preparations. In the 1950s, nuclear submarines started prowling the oceans and were faster than the destroyer escorts Canada built to hunt them after World War II. It was decided to retrofit these ships with helicopters, hangars, and landing pads. This model tested how these modifications affected ship performance.

Research models are kin to other forms of scientific craftwork. Like museum dioramas and botanical models with removeable parts, they are handmade by builders with traditional skills. The wind-tunnel models, for example, are constructed using the bread-and-butter technique, the layering of wood slices (the bread) and glue (the butter).

As is typical with institutional models, we don't know who fashioned them. Like so many other anonymous makers, builders of research models belong to the guild of "invisible technicians," the band of artificers who have, over the centuries, crafted instruments, apparatus, and models for scientists, enabling experimentation, observation, and measurement. Models may perform different work in different spaces, but together they embody the crafting and tinkering embedded in science, and—much like these photographs—the sleight-of-hand fun in playing with scale.

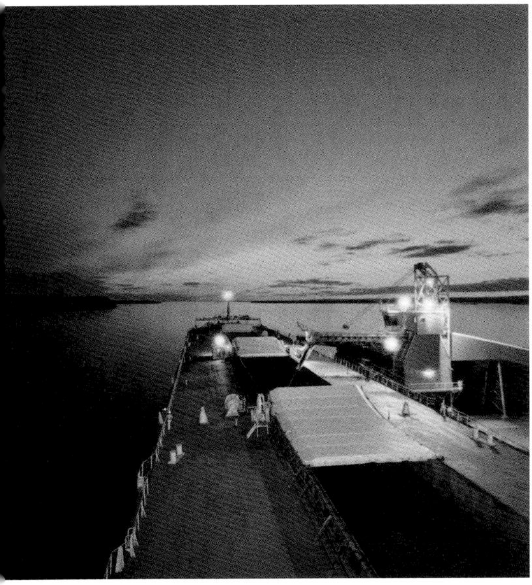
Gulf of St. Lawrence, 2002

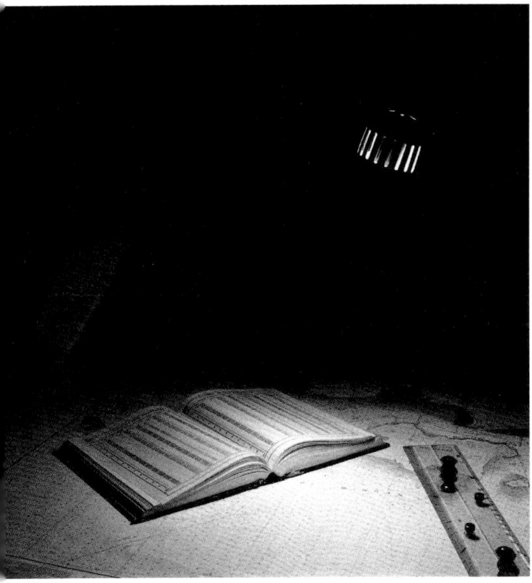
Gulf of St. Lawrence, 2002

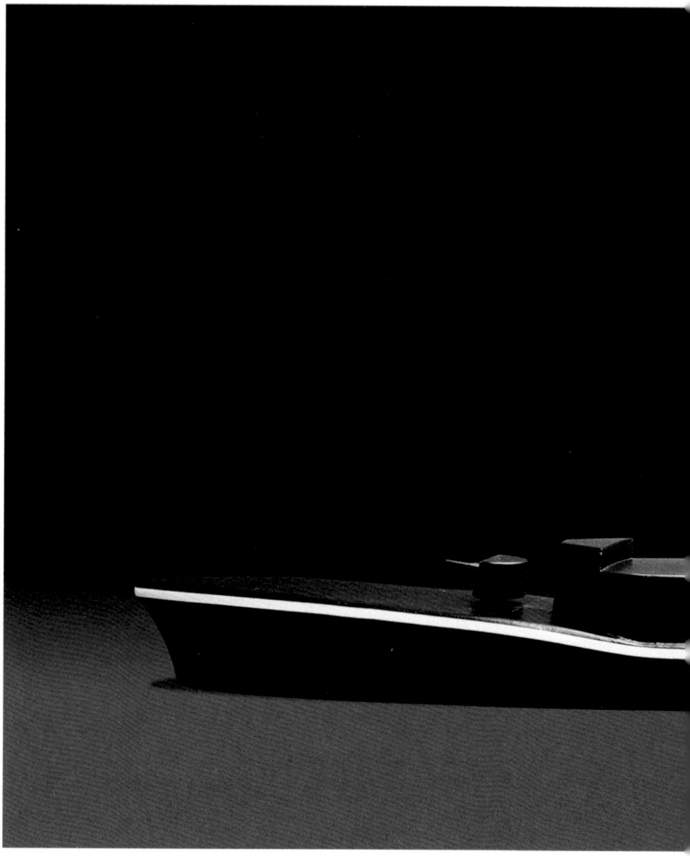

DESTROYER ESCORT, WIND-TUNNEL MODEL

National Research Council of Canada
1990.0029, Ingenium, Ottawa, Ontario

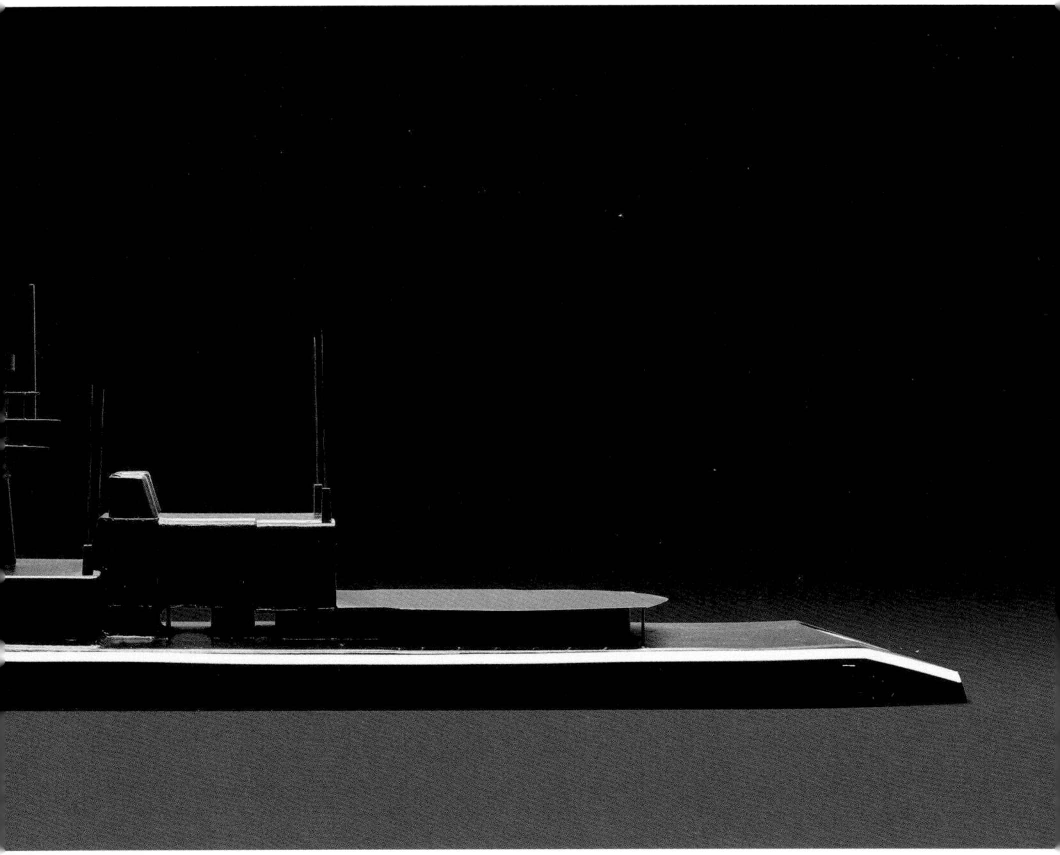

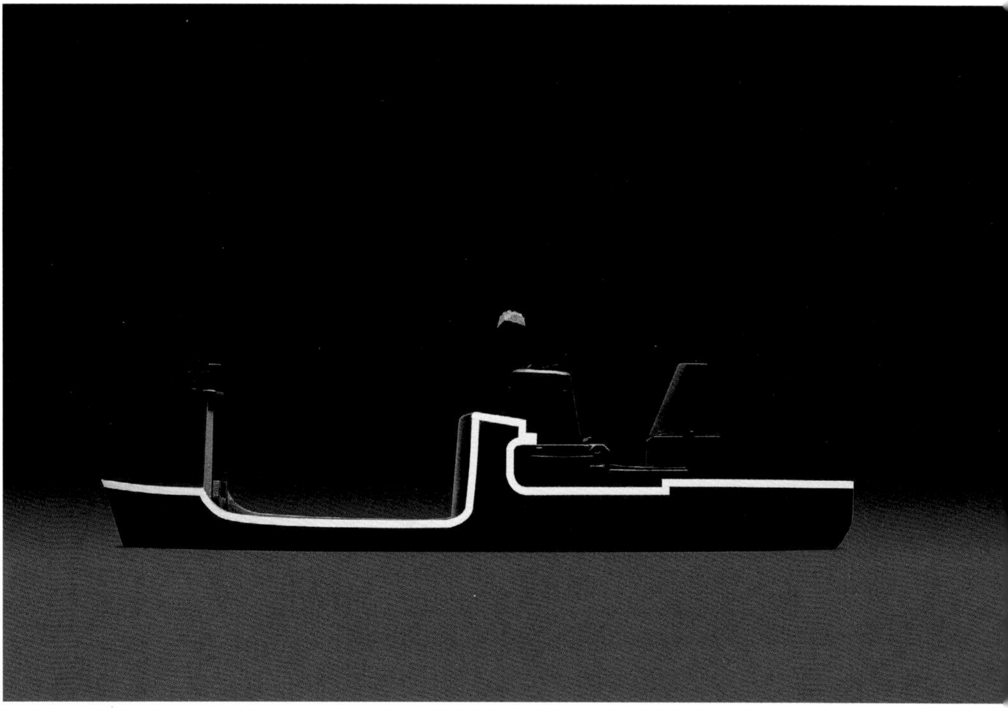

BUOY TENDER, WIND-TUNNEL MODEL

National Research Council of Canada
1990.0030, Ingenium, Ottawa, Ontario

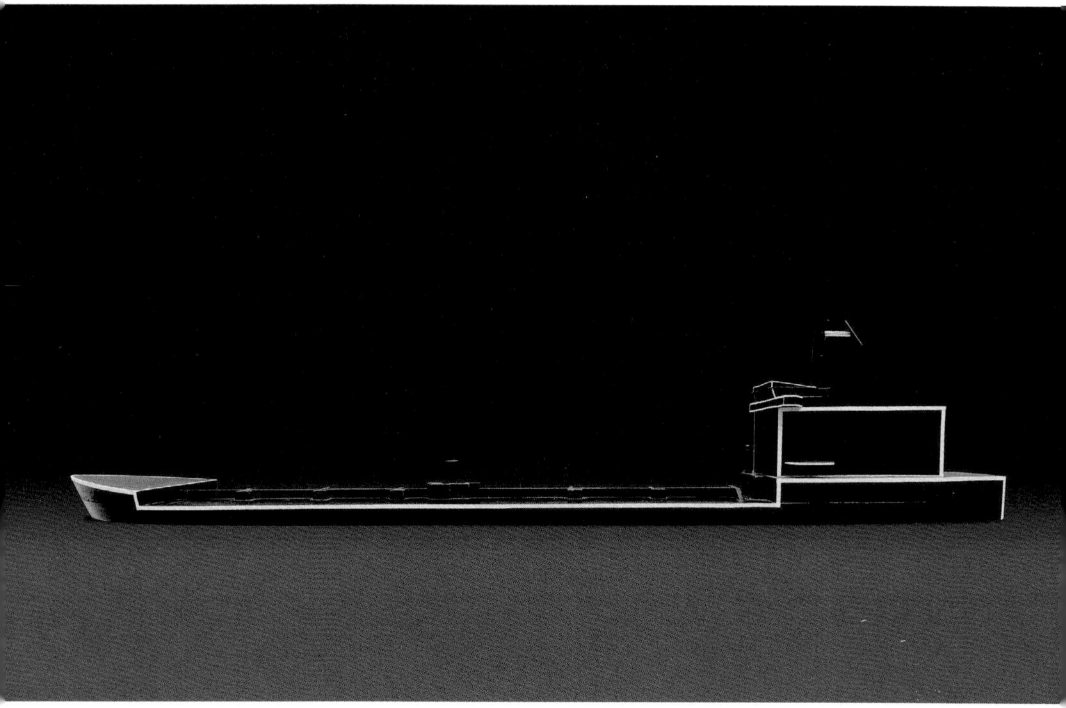

OIL TANKER, WIND-TUNNEL MODEL

National Research Council of Canada
1990.0031, Ingenium, Ottawa, Ontario

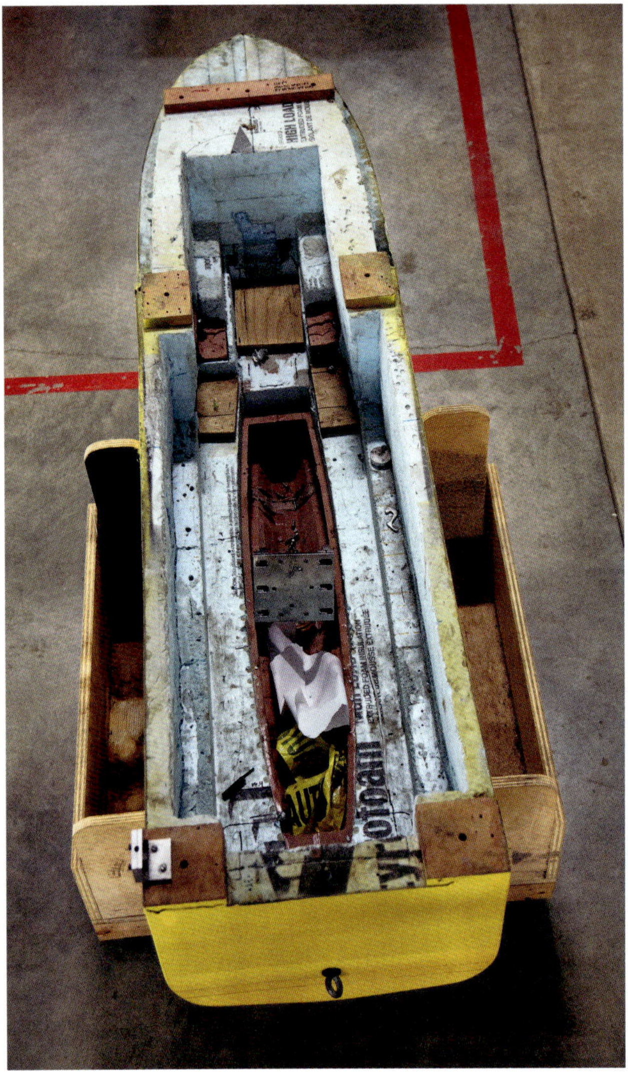

MEMORIAL UNIVERSITY TOWING TANK MODEL

Oceanic Consulting Corporation, Newfoundland and Labrador

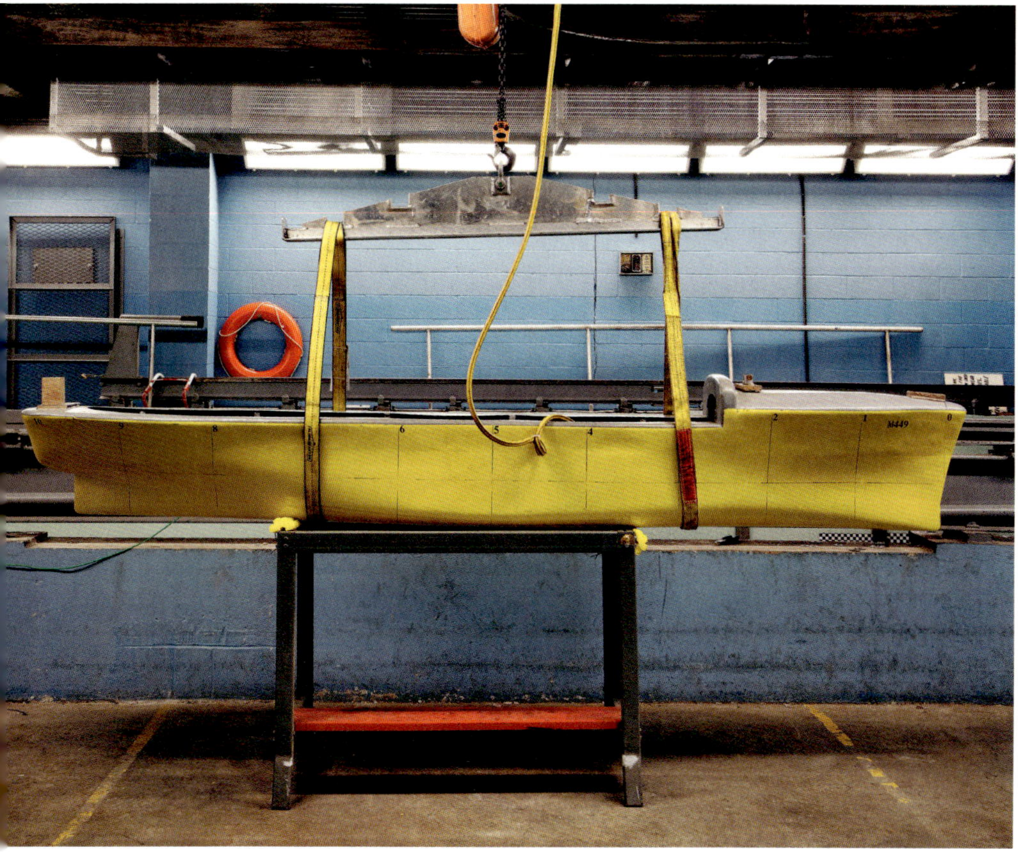

"M499," MEMORIAL UNIVERSITY TOWING TANK MODEL

National Research Council Canada

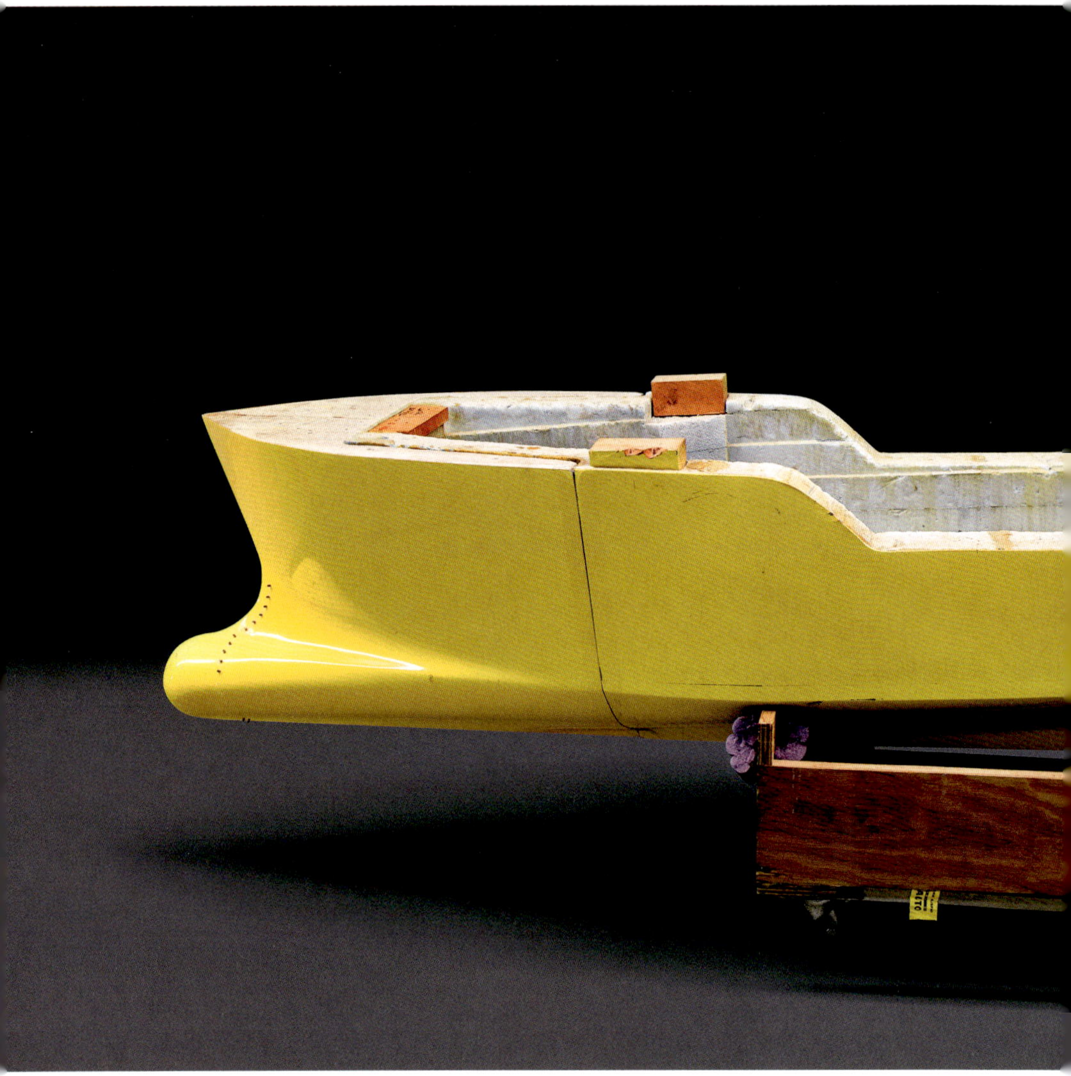

MEMORIAL UNIVERSITY TOWING TANK MODEL

Oceanic Consulting Corporation, Newfoundland and Labrador

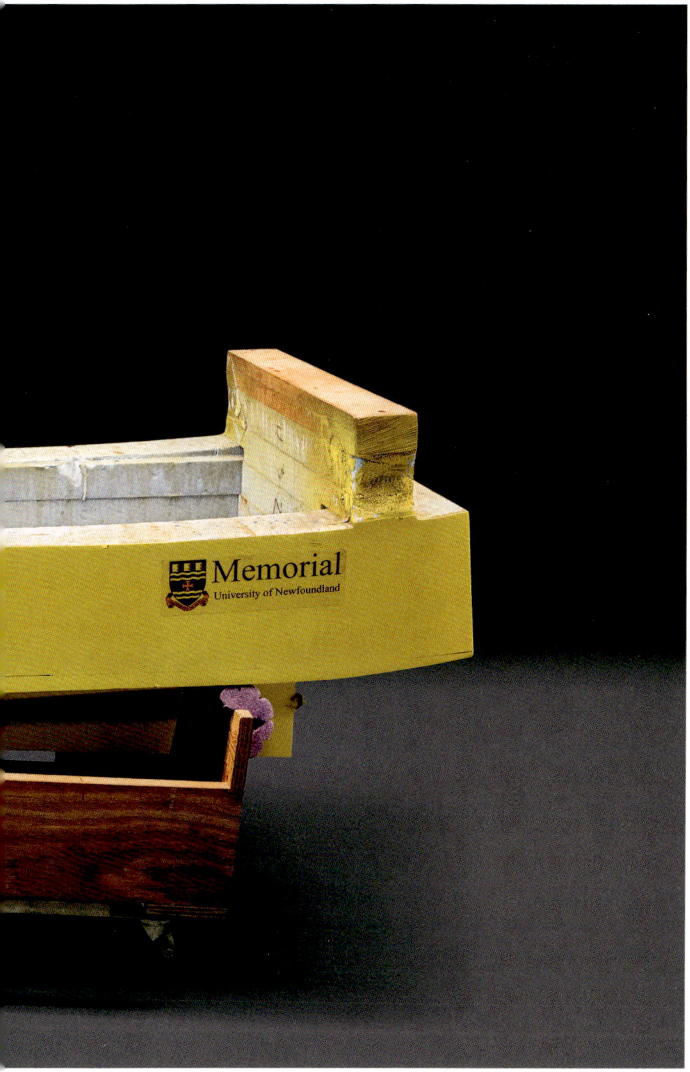
Memorial
University of Newfoundland

ALONE IN MY WORKSHOP

ROBERT MELLIN
Architect
Model Owner
Writer

Tilting,
Fogo Island
and St. John's,
Newfoundland and Labrador

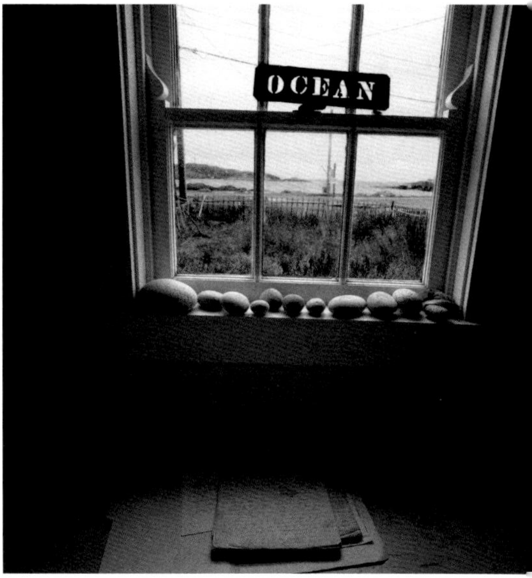

Fogo Island, Newfoundland and Labrador, 2004

I collected several model boats for my house in Tilting on Fogo Island, an intact vernacular structure from 1888, that I love and always return to. These models remind me of their makers and of my own life messing among artifacts and all things particular to Newfoundland.

I have several models by Raymond Bursey: punts and longliners. His models are scaled proportionally and accurately to the vessels of Fogo Island. Raymond built a harbour scene in an open tank, replete with boats floating in water, wharves, lifts, sheds, and a fish processing plant, a tribute to his working life at what's now called the Fogo Island Co-operative.

I also own two models purchased from a gentleman I met in St. John's. His models are not accurate in scale. Their hulls are made of balsa wood, with curves shaped and accentuated through the addition of plaster. The masts are straight dowel rods, anchored with the type of white string common to butcher stores of the past. His models were created with limited means and materials that were readily available. What intrigues me is the connection between this model maker—I can't remember his name—retired from fishing and living alone in the city, and his models, viscerally connected to memories of real fishing boats, from an outport community abandoned in the mid-1900s when the government resettlement program turned lives upside down.

People sometimes draw maps based on their memories of a place, not technically accurate maps but more like cognitive maps with distortions that emphasize certain features. Models are often conceived in a similar manner. Perfection is not the goal, and the unusual results are more interesting to me than most meticulously crafted examples.

EILEEN NEWMAN

Daughter of Raymond Bursey

Fogo Island,
Newfoundland and Labrador

My dad was Raymond Bursey. He retired when he was 55 because he had a bad back. That was when he got into model boats. Before that he was the manager of the Fogo Island Marine Centre and operated the boat lift.

He made no big deal of his models. He did small ones; he did big ones. He made longliners, schooners, and other fishing boats. He packed them up and sent them to people who wanted them. My brother says there was one model that you could take the top part off. Mom made little quilts and pillows for the bunks inside.

Yes, we wish we had more of his boats. He did one each for his grandchildren, but I never did have one for a long time. But I got one now, from a business owner on the island who died and passed his on.

Dad was all about details. Any time we went to St. John's, he had a list of things to pick up from the store. He worked by himself in his shed. He was all focus, no music. He built a wharf scene in a wooden box for his front garden. He had the concrete wall next to the driveway painted with a scene of icebergs, fishing boats, and stages. He had it repainted after it got weather-beaten.

Dad was born in Gander Bay. His father died when he was seven or eight. It was a big family, so he was one of the three oldest sent to the orphanage in St. John's. When he was 12, he had two choices. There was a lighthouse keeper and his wife who would have taken him on Change Islands, but he wouldn't be able to go to school. So, he ended up with a married couple on Fogo Island.

Dad would say to our grandson, oh, my, Damien, I wouldn't like you to have it so hard as what I did. He went out fishing when he was 13 and the man from Fogo kept his paycheque and locked the pantry door. He had a hard upbringing but survived all that. In later years he was in touch with all his family. His sister just turned 88, and my dad died in 2022.

Raymond Bursey, Model Maker, Fogo Island, Newfoundland and Labrador. Photographs Bursey & Newman Families

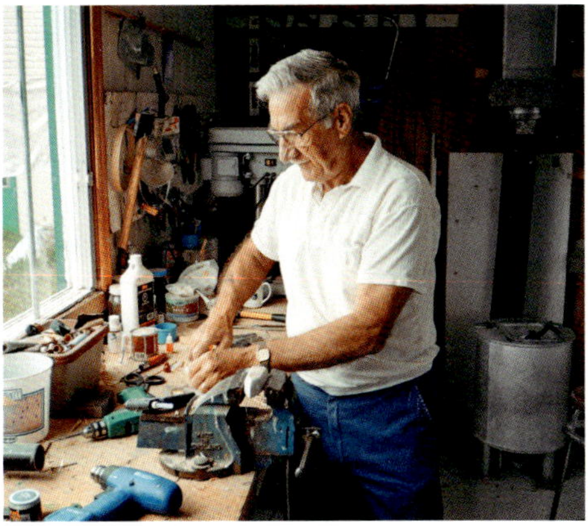

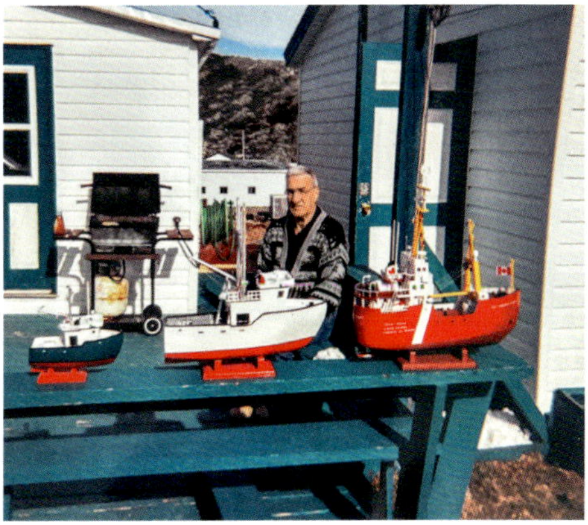

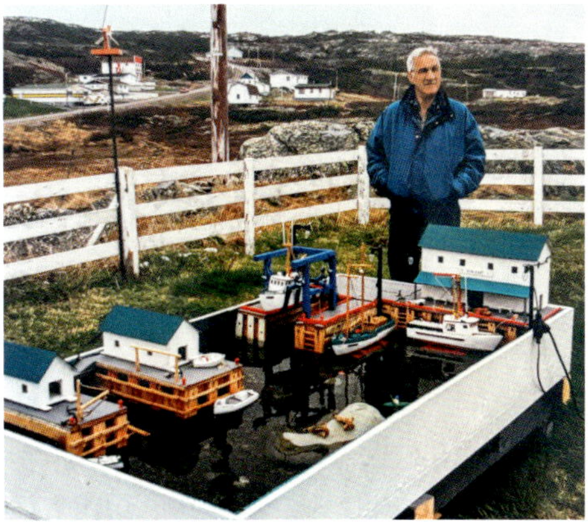

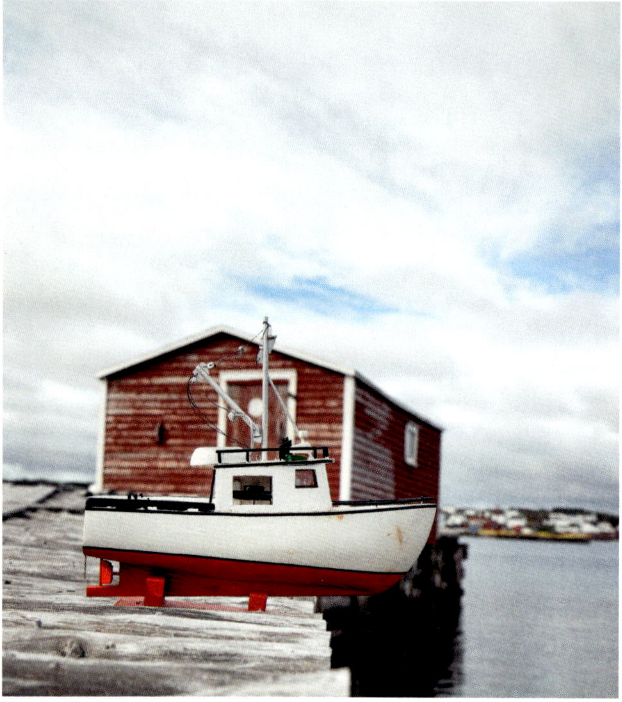

LONGLINER

Raymond Bursey, Fogo Island, Newfoundland and Labrador

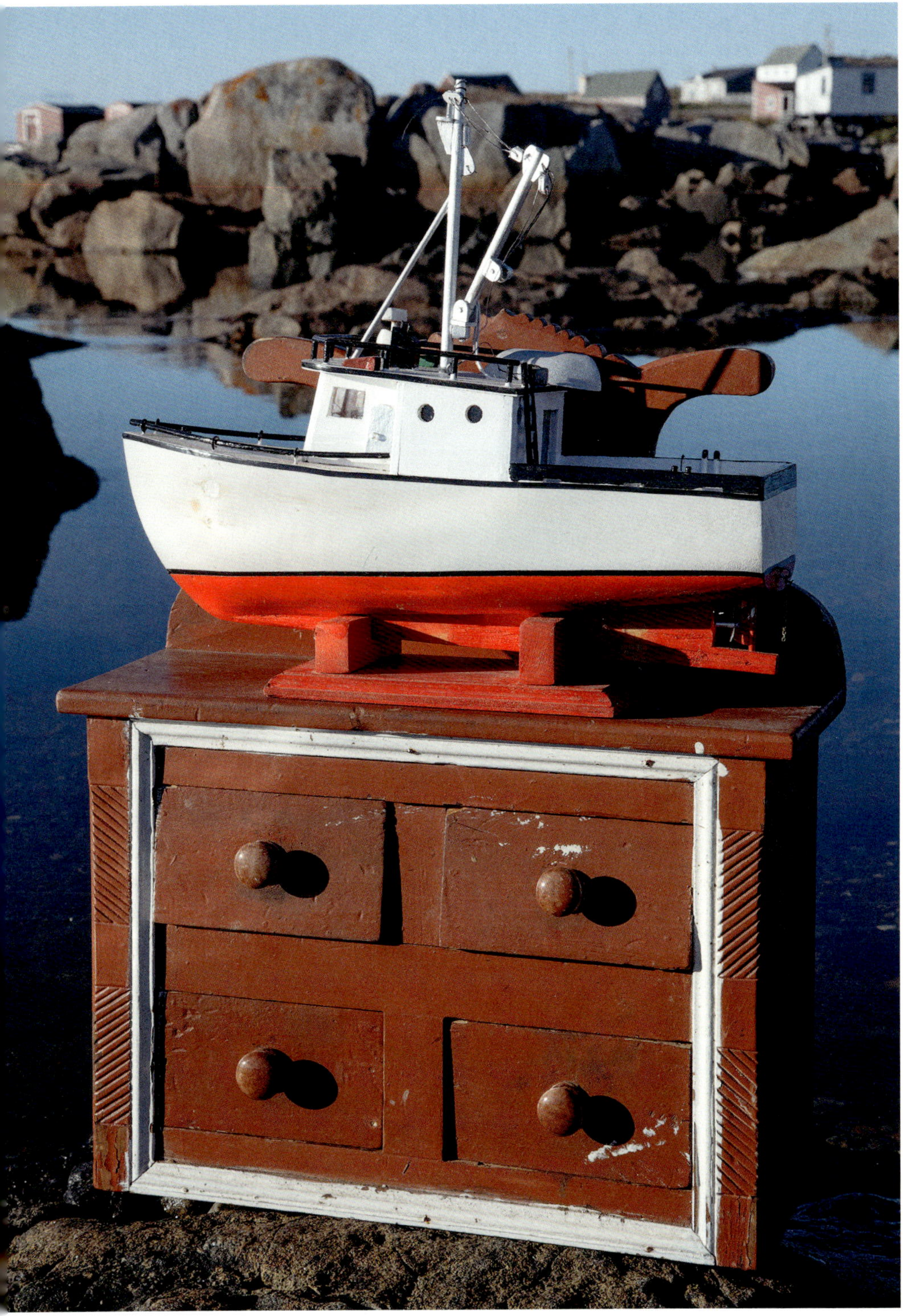

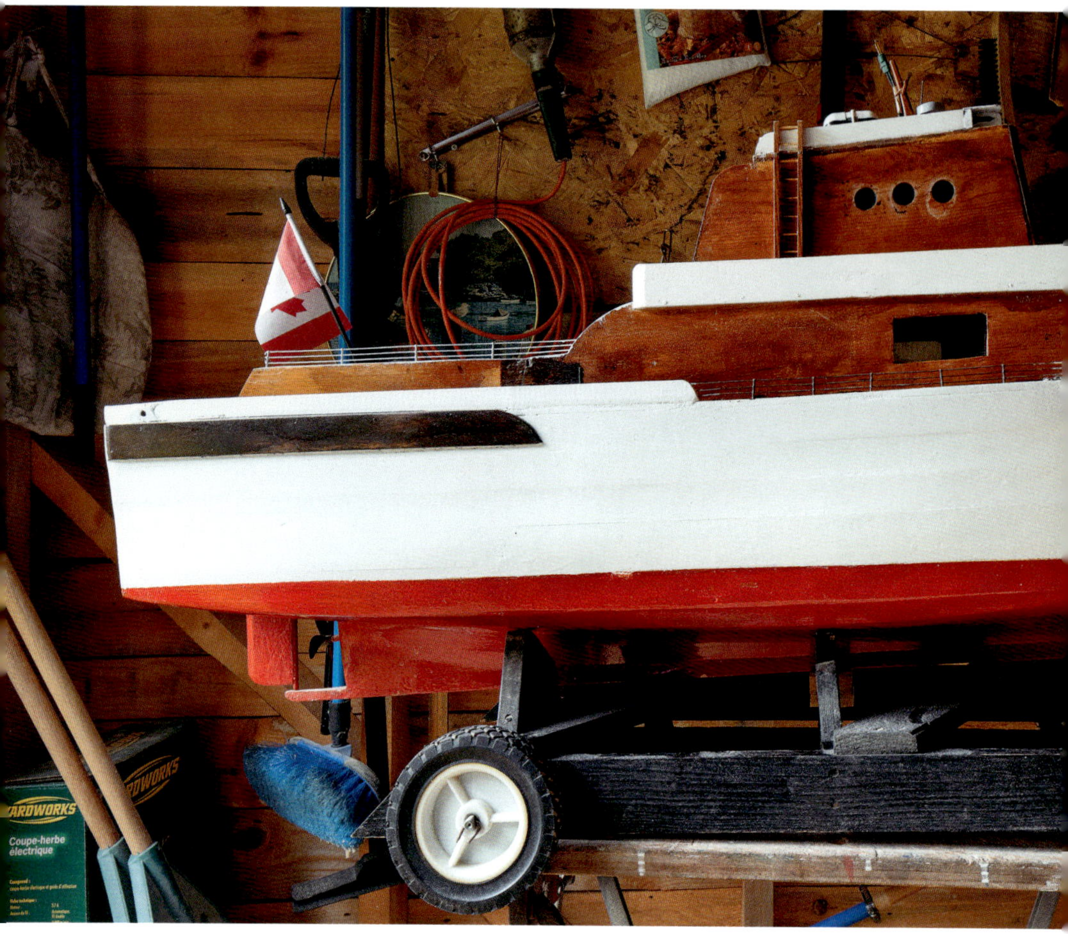

"MY DREAM," CABIN CRUISER

Carson Welch, Newcombville, Nova Scotia

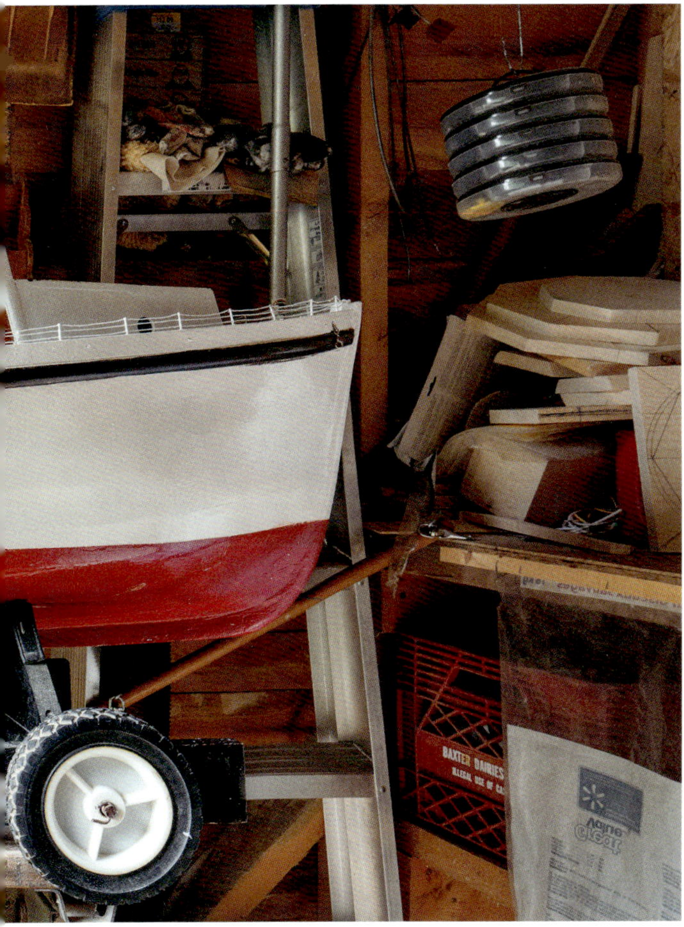
BAXTER DAIRIES

OLD DORY, NEW DORY

Sidney Mahaney & Milford Buchanan,
Nova Scotia Shelburne Museum Dory Shop, Nova Scotia

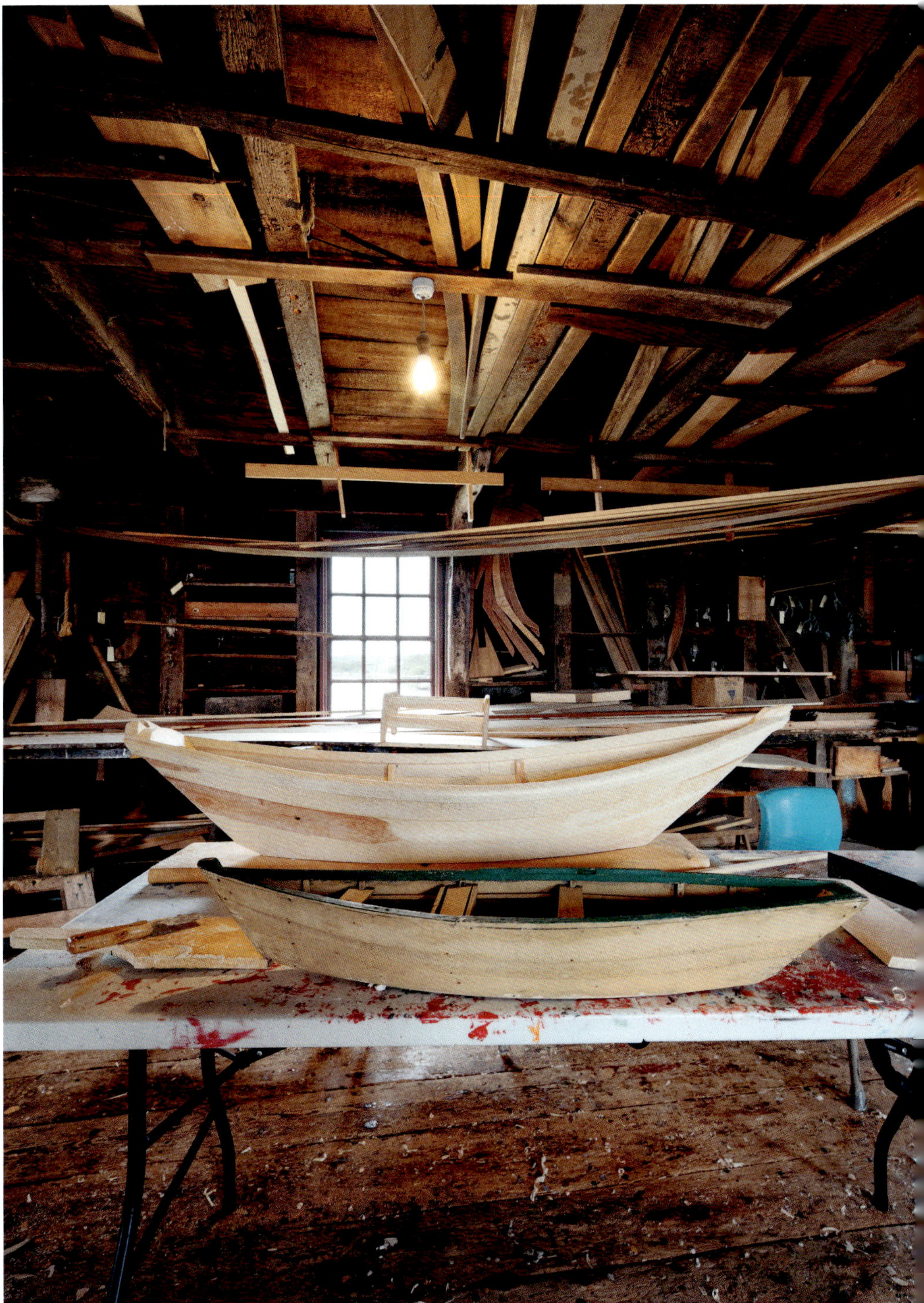

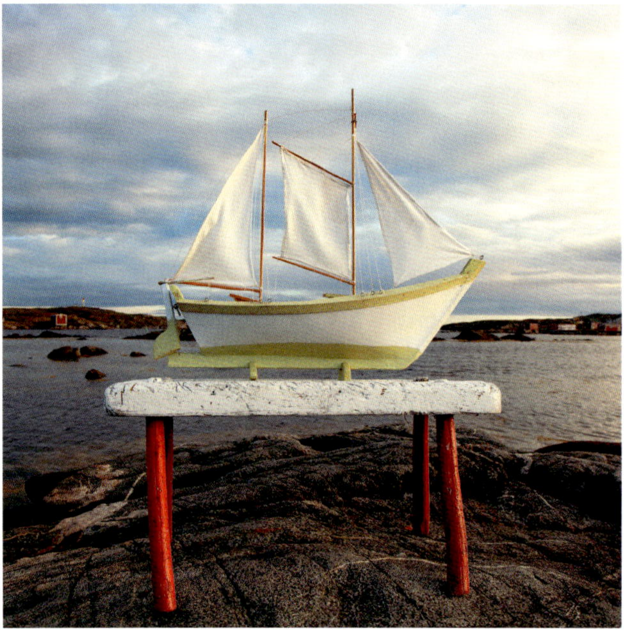

TWO-MASTED SCHOONER

Maker unknown, Newfoundland and Labrador

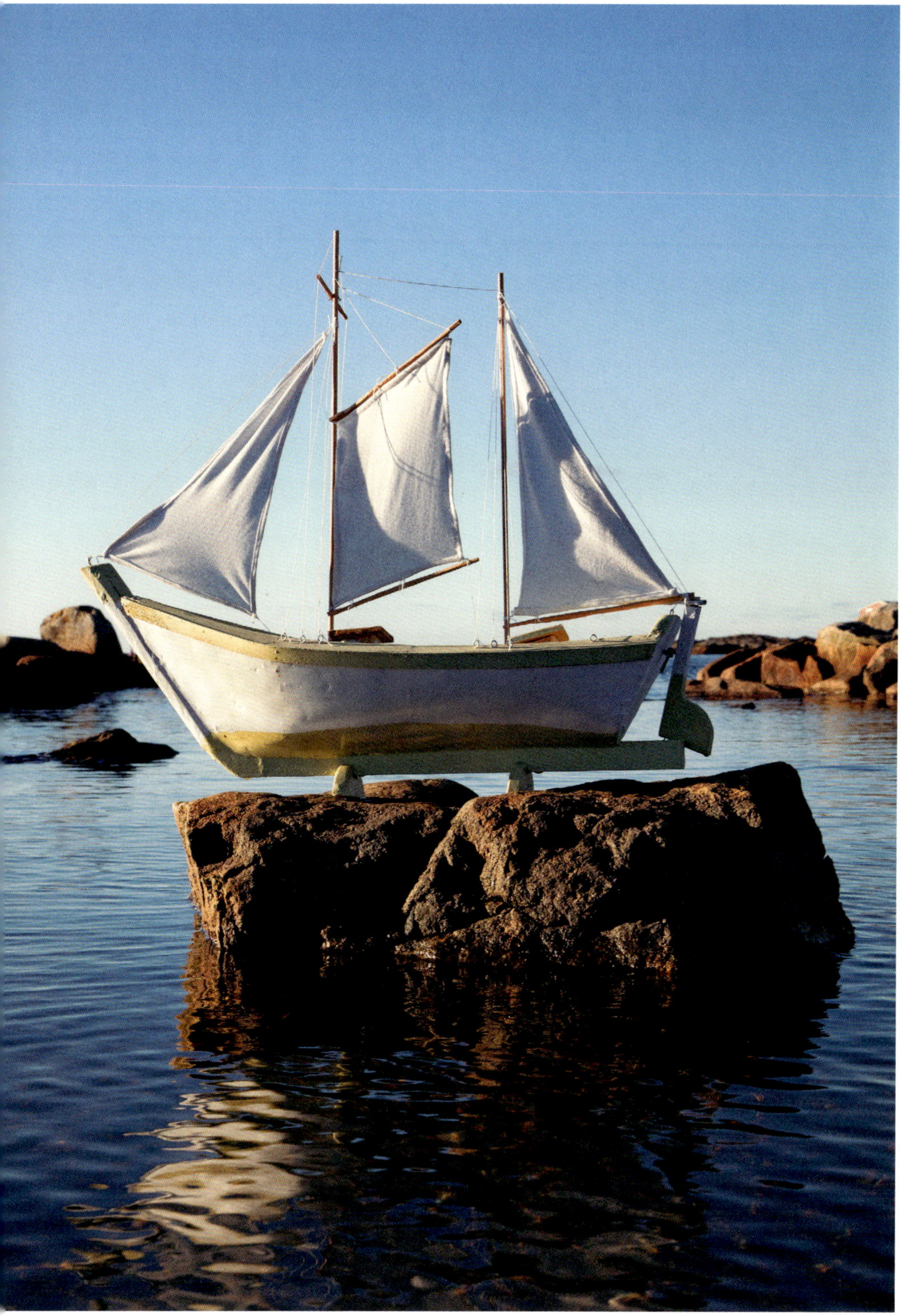

"CHETICAMP," STERN TRAWLER

Maker unknown, Nova Scotia

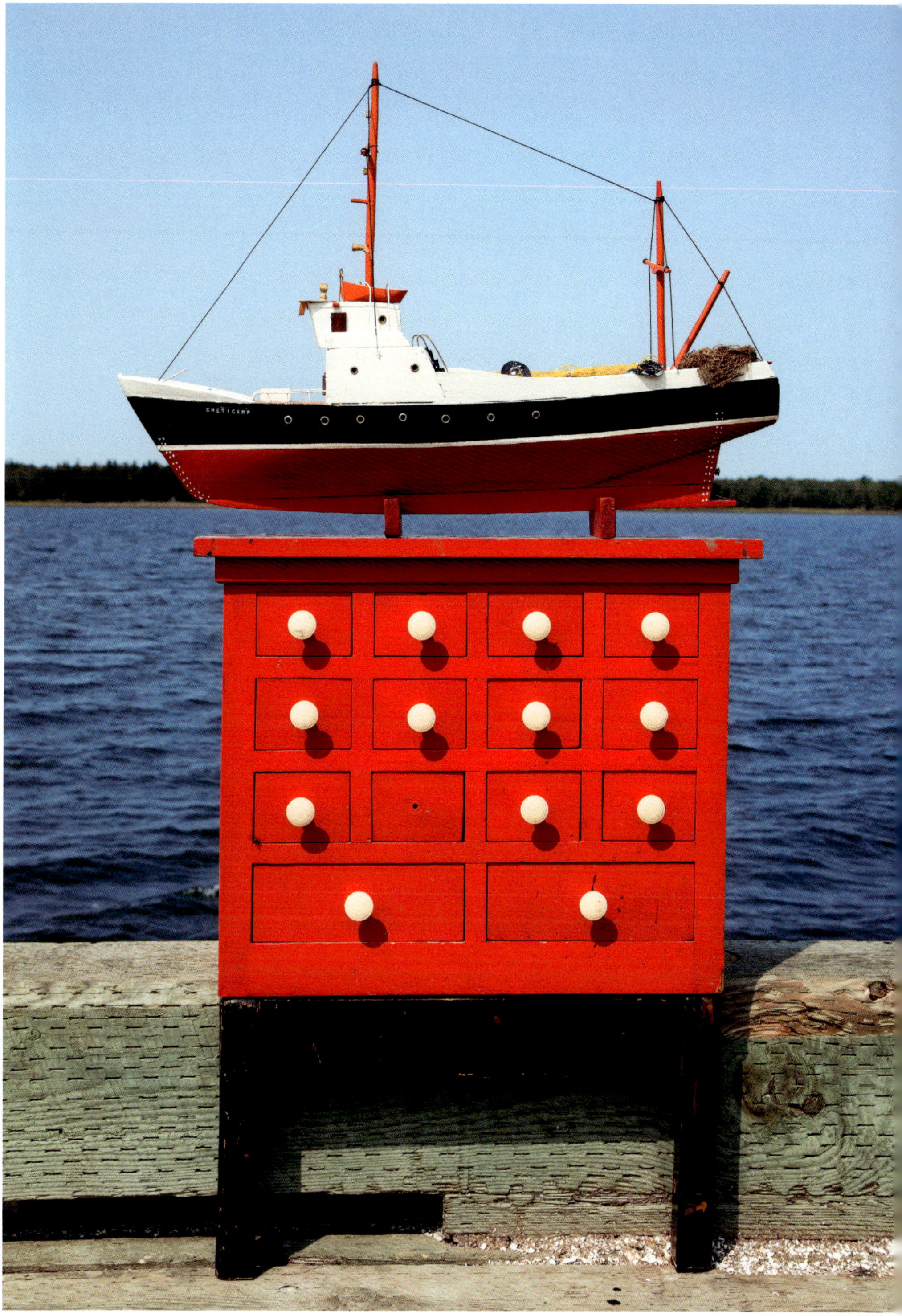
CHÉTICAMP

LONGLINER

Maker unknown, Newfoundland and Labrador

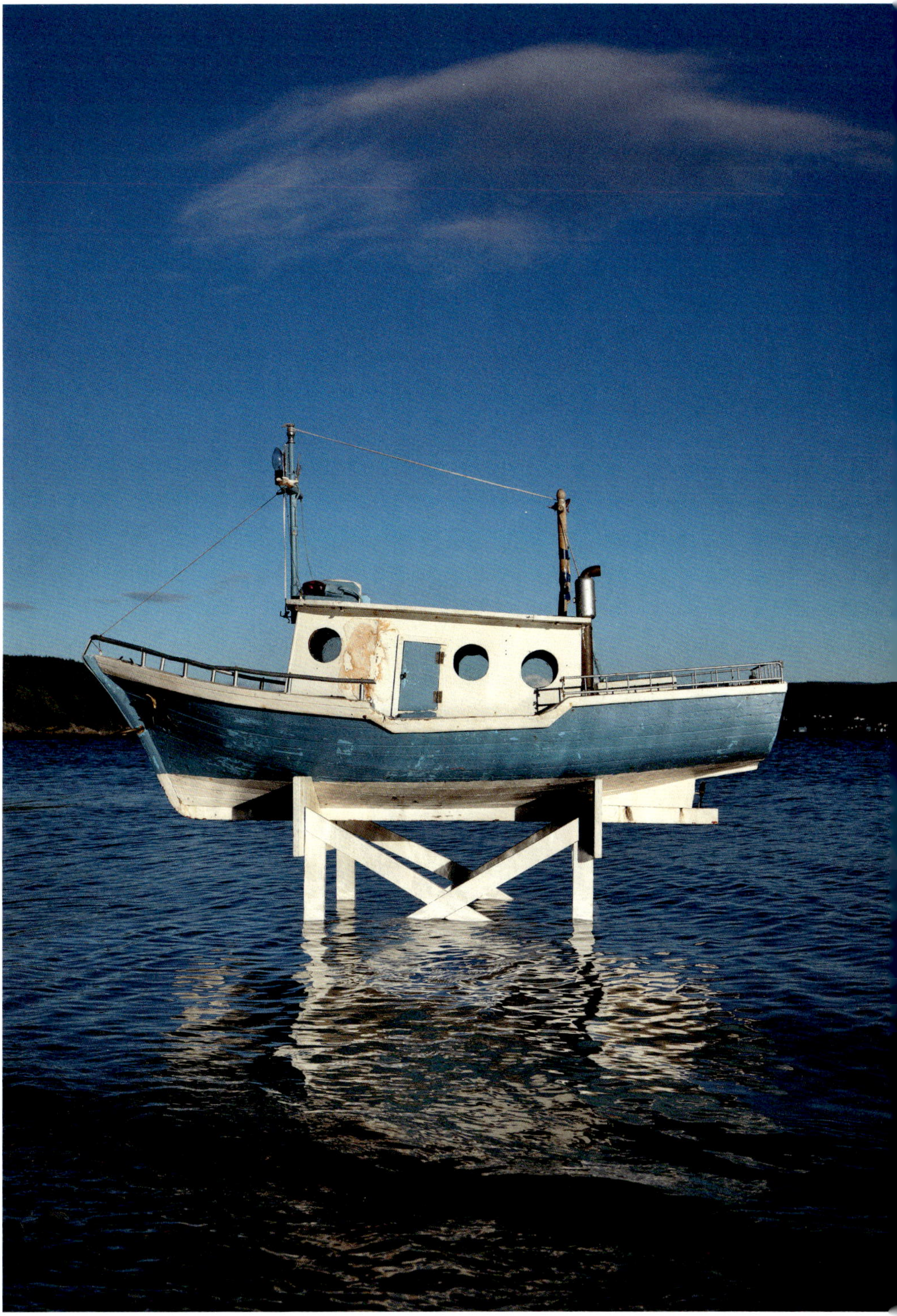

PRESERVING HISTORY

MARK BOUDREAU

Model Maker

Port Hawkesbury,
Cape Breton Island,
Nova Scotia

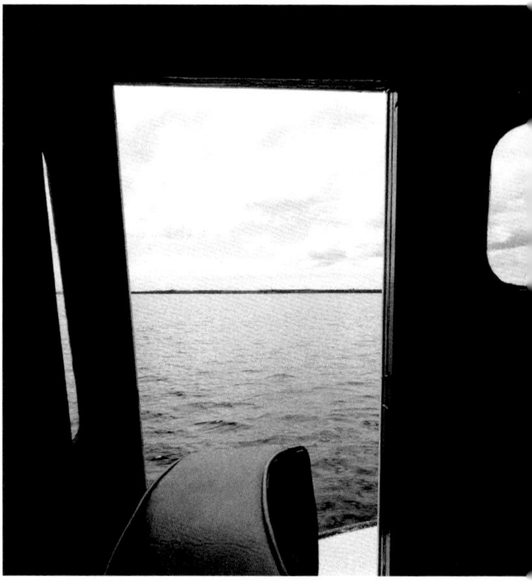

Caribou Harbour, Nova Scotia, 2002

I was born in 1937, and I grew up speaking French in Boudreauville, Cape Breton Island. My dad worked on a coastal boat, the "Surf," from the 1930s up to wartime. I think he was getting 50 cents a day. The "Surf" was built as a yacht, fuelled by a coal steam engine, all brass and mahogany, built for a rich American. It was used for rum running and seized by the American government during prohibition. Wentworth MacDonald, owner of the Margaree Steamship Company of Sydney, bought it. He had boats going everywhere, the Bras d'Or Lake, Arichat, Mulgrave, Port Hawkesbury, running with passengers and freight. He would go as far as PEI for potatoes.

One crew always stayed on the "Surf" over the weekends to keep the boilers warm. When it was my dad's turn, my mom and I would hop on. Just the three of us on that 200-foot boat. I used to enjoy looking at those engine rods going up and down. We had the whole boat to ourselves. It was only me and my mother and dad there.

My grandfather had a fish plant, John Landry's fish plant. They used to salt a lot of fish. You'd salt the haddock, the mackerel, the cod, the hake, whatever came in there. I remember I worked on the weekends and they used to get some haul; they made boxes to put the fish in, cut the head off of them, iced them up, and shipped them out. You'd take the head home and you would get a couple of good feeds out of it. And they had a lobster-canning plant upstairs. There was a bunch of ladies taking the lobsters out of the shell and packing it in cans. In them days they had the old washing machine wringers, that's what they used to get the meat out of the claws. Just put 'em through that, squeeze 'em out.

I was 17 when I made my first model. It didn't take me long to find out that I had to get them a little more professional. You just put the blueprints on the wall, and you work right off that. Same as building a house.

I'm not interested in sailing ships, only steam, motors, working boats. I wouldn't build a boat unless it had history to it. I had the addresses of all the archives in the world and I would write one letter, make copies, and send them along everywhere. I was looking for pictures and plans—I used to make all my own small parts, everything you need on a vessel. The "Queen Mary" needed quite a few lifeboats; you make an original and then you make a mould.

A couple of years ago this guy was looking for steamship models. He called the museum in Halifax, and they gave him my name. My daughter Colleen sent him some pictures and then he called and said, yes, that's what he wanted. He was buying models for a man who wanted to make a travelling exhibition. He sent a cheque, and I called a furniture mover and away they went to Ontario; seven models all at 3/16th inch to a foot scale. Colleen tried to visit the models on display, but there was never any information. I don't know where they're at. Sooner or later, they'll pop up. The SS "Glencoe" was part of the Newfoundland Alphabet fleet, for the letter G. The SS "Kyle" steamship ran aground in Harbour Grace, Newfoundland. The Coast Guard ship, "Walter E. Foster," supplied lighthouses and set buoys. The steamer "Hurry On" hit a wave in the Strait of Canso. Water got in the hatch, the load shifted, and it sank. That was 1935, before the causeway was built. Some crew went down with the boat, some froze on the lifeboat, and seven came ashore in Judique.

When I was working, it would probably take me a year or two to build one model. After I retired, I could build two in one year. I sold maybe 75 boats, and 42 of them were museum pieces. The Halifax Museum had two or three of them there for a long time, including the "Titanic." Now the "Titanic," that's built at a 1/16th scale. That's small, but the model itself is six feet long. If you built it bigger than that, you couldn't fit it in a living room.

I quit making models five years ago—it's done and over. I'm still as steady as can be, but you can get sick, you can start shaking, and you get tired after a while too. Nobody will finish a model if you leave it. The only one we have is the "Surf," and it's at my son's. He just finished a new home, so I said, Garnet, your house is done, finished. Take this model, get it out of here. So he's got it, ten minutes down the road.

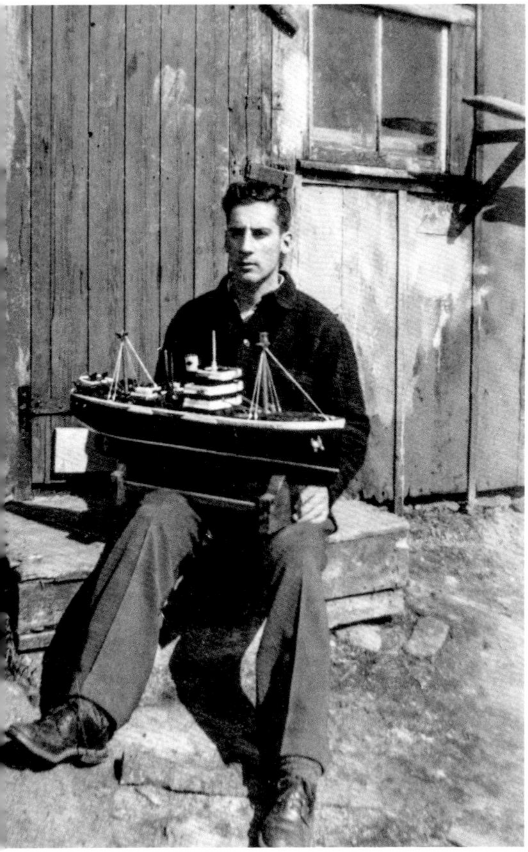

Mark Boudreau & "Wabana," 1954
Photograph Boudreau Family

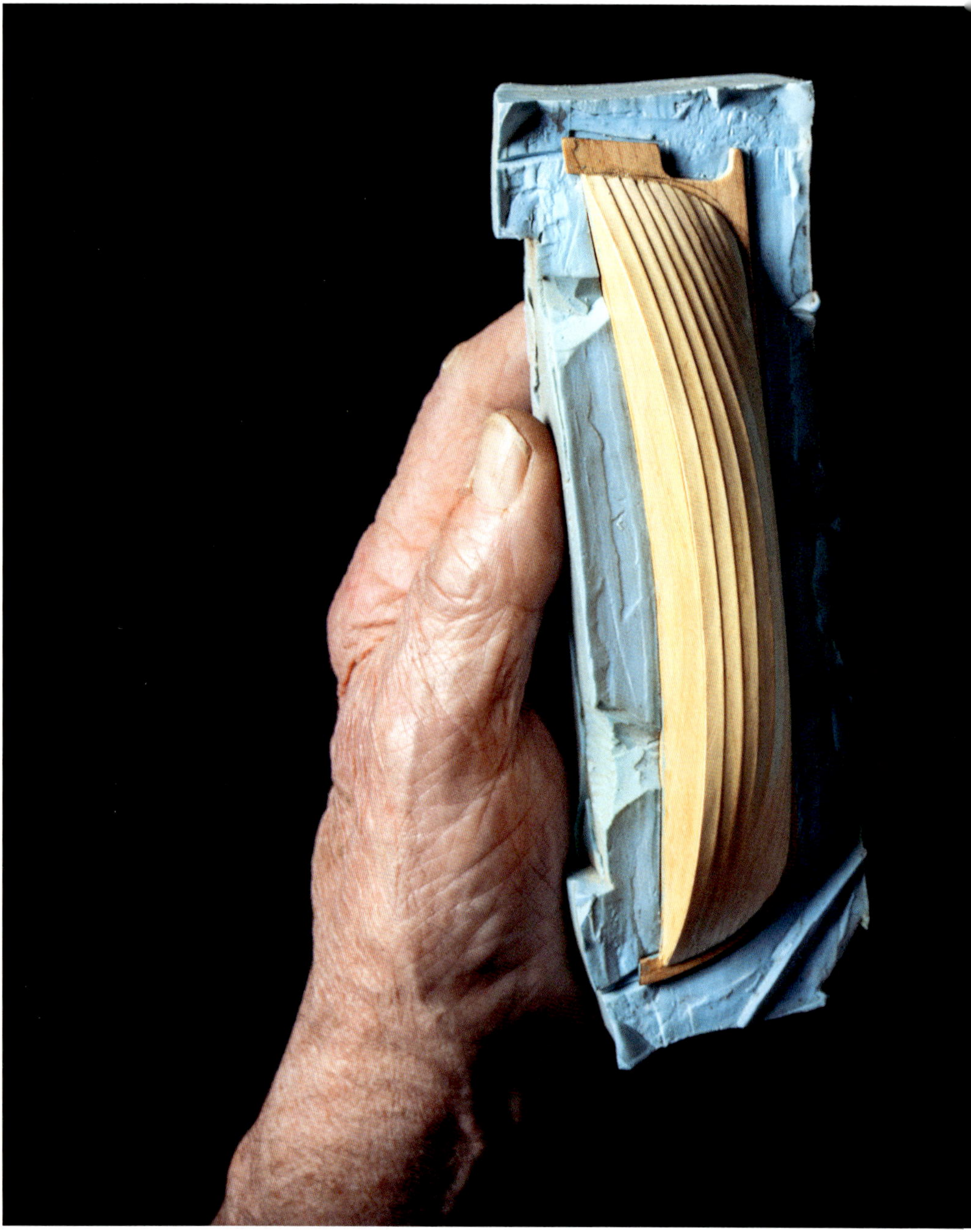

LIFEBOAT & MOULD

Mark Boudreau, Port Hawkesbury, Nova Scotia

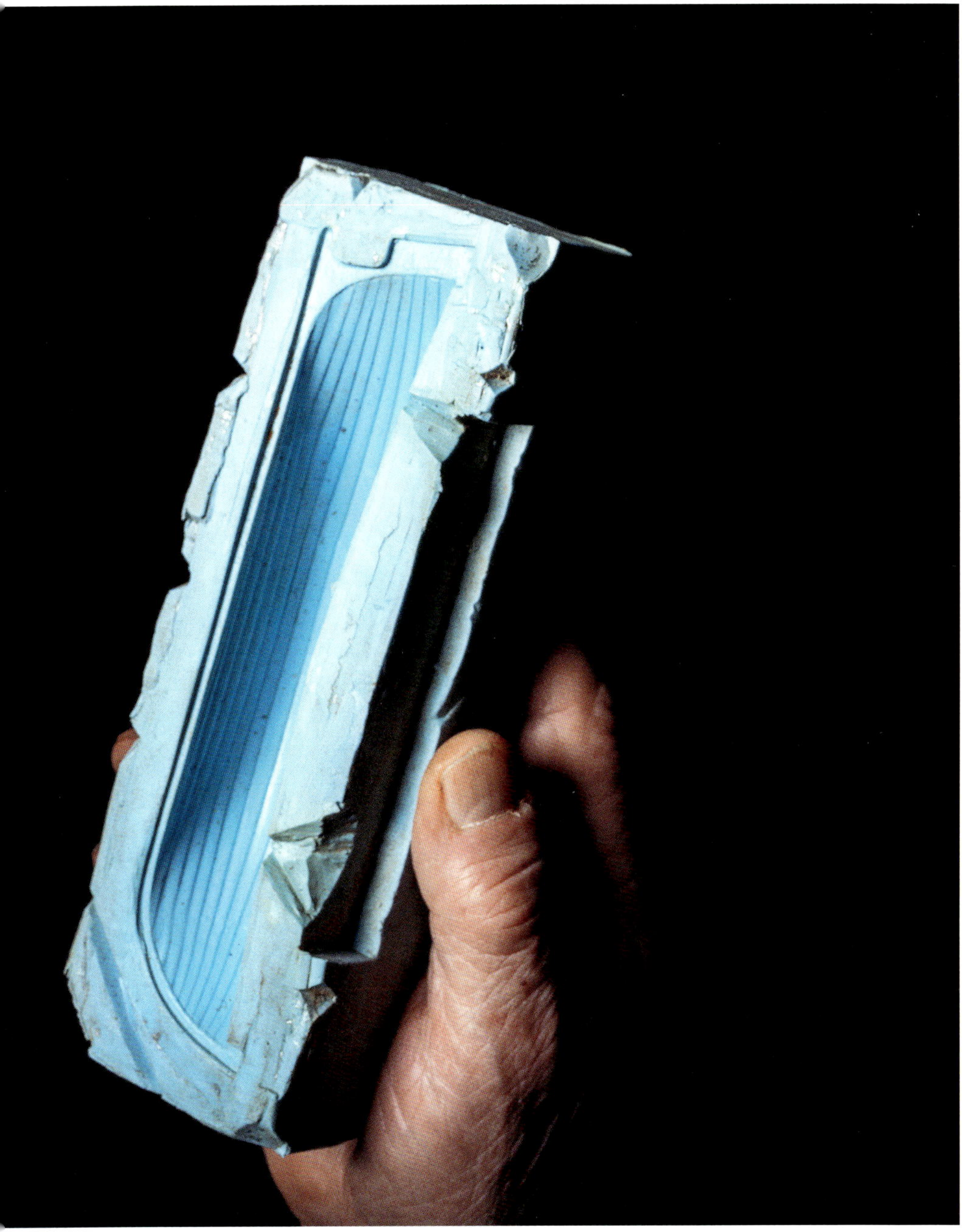

GREG HILTZ

Model Maker

Baxter's Corner,
New Brunswick

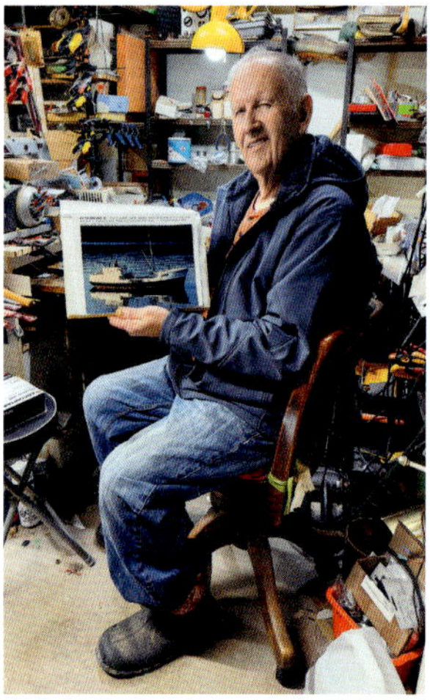

Greg Hiltz, with image of remote-controlled model, "Adventurer II"
Baxters Corner, New Brunswick

I'm a fisherman's son, so I grew up around boats. I was born in Halls Harbour on the Bay of Fundy shore. When I was seven my father moved us all down to Church Point, Nova Scotia, where there were more boats, more lobsters, more fish. My first model boat was a replica of a lobster fishing boat carved from a wooden fishing buoy. I was 12 or 14 years old, and I had the most rudimentary tools to work with. My second was a model of my father's fishing boat, the "Zoe T." I started getting compliments on my model making, so I continued from there.

My favourite model to build was the "Adventurer II," an offshore scallop dragger, built by A.F. Theriault & Son in Meteghan River. That model took me 2,350 hours to build. I built it quite large scale, 44 inches long. I also went the extra mile and made it completely radio controlled to sail in the water with propulsion and rudder control. I had 23 mini lights on it, a rotating radar, and all that stuff that was popular in the hobby. That's the crowning touch, to see your model act the way a real one does in the water, and you have full control of it as if you are in the wheelhouse.

When the "Adventurer II" was finished, I took it down to the Theriault shipyard. The owner, executives, and staff all wanted it for their booth at a fishery show. Would I be willing to rent or lease it to the shipyard if it was insured? I took it to a professional model builder who used what's called the Smithsonian criteria to appraise it. His appraisal come back that if he had to reproduce my model based on my degree of detail and standards, then he would charge $29,500, which completely blew me away. They did insure it and they put it in their trade shows.

About a year after I made the "Adventurer II," Connors Brothers in Blacks Harbour, New Brunswick, contacted me. They are the biggest sardine company in Canada. Connors had seven sardine and herring carrier boats they wanted to reproduce in model size. Then it hit me: I was preserving a

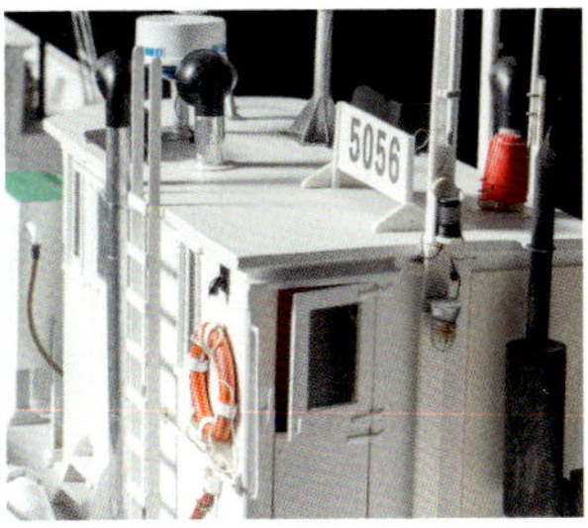

"Brunswick Maid" (detail)

history. I went down to Blacks Harbour, and the "Brunswick Maid" was hauled up. It had been modified from a schooner design in 1921, and now it was decommissioned. There were no blueprints. Anyway, I made a very crude carpenter square from wood that was basically 10 feet by 8 feet. I went aboard that weekend, and all day I transferred measurements from the real boat to paper. If I can get every curve, every dip of that hull from stem to stern, I can produce plans to make a model.

Having the blueprint gives you what's called the hull lines plan. You transfer those plans to wood, cut them, assemble them like a jigsaw puzzle, and then build it from there. I have collected over 160 sets of shipyard blueprints. I supply those to people for the cost of copying. Blueprints keep more people in the hobby.

For 25 years, I was the go-to guy for plans and technical advice for Lowell Briggs Hobbies in Comeauville, Nova Scotia. When the owner turned 71, he said, Greg, I'm going to retire. So bottom line, I bought out a model boat shop. I call myself Greg's Model Boatyard. What fit into the Lowell Briggs shop, which was 25 by 30 feet, is now crammed into a bedroom 12 feet by 12 feet. How long do I want to keep on? I might not keep the store, but I hope to build models until the day I keel over and die.

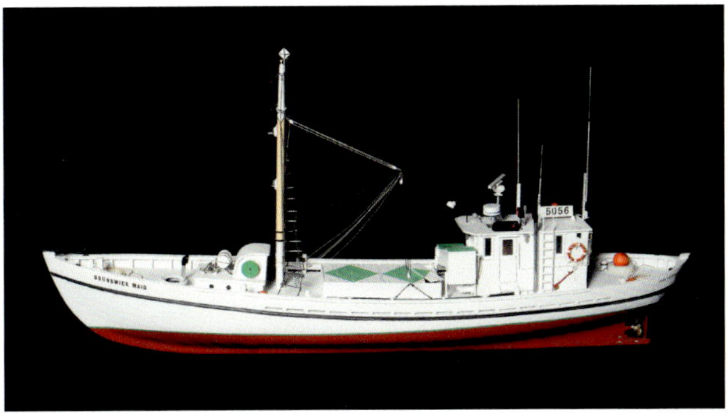

"Brunswick Maid," Herring Carrier
Greg Hiltz, Baxters Corner, New Brunswick

"JACKIE T," TUG

John Lyle, Chester Basin, Nova Scotia

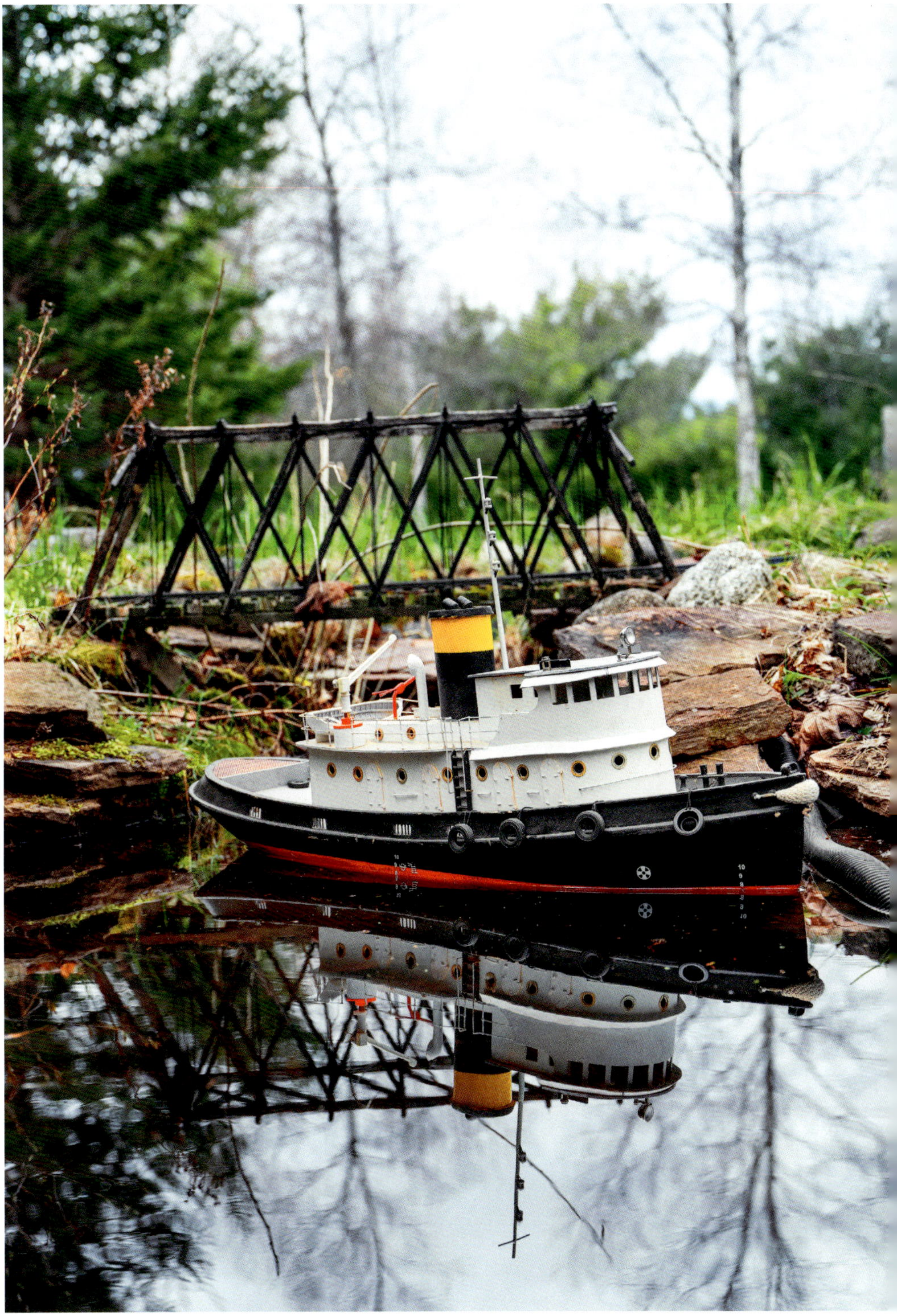

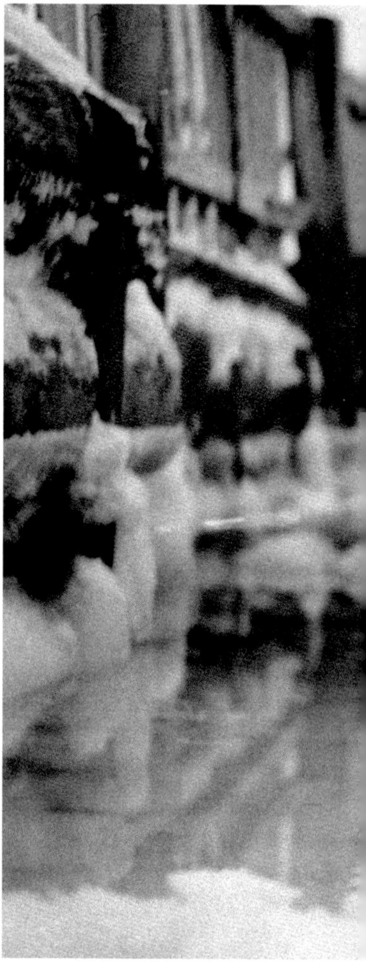

"TRUSTY," STEAM TUG

21-inch working model, 1930

Buckley Family Nova Scotia Archives 1985-386 no. 687

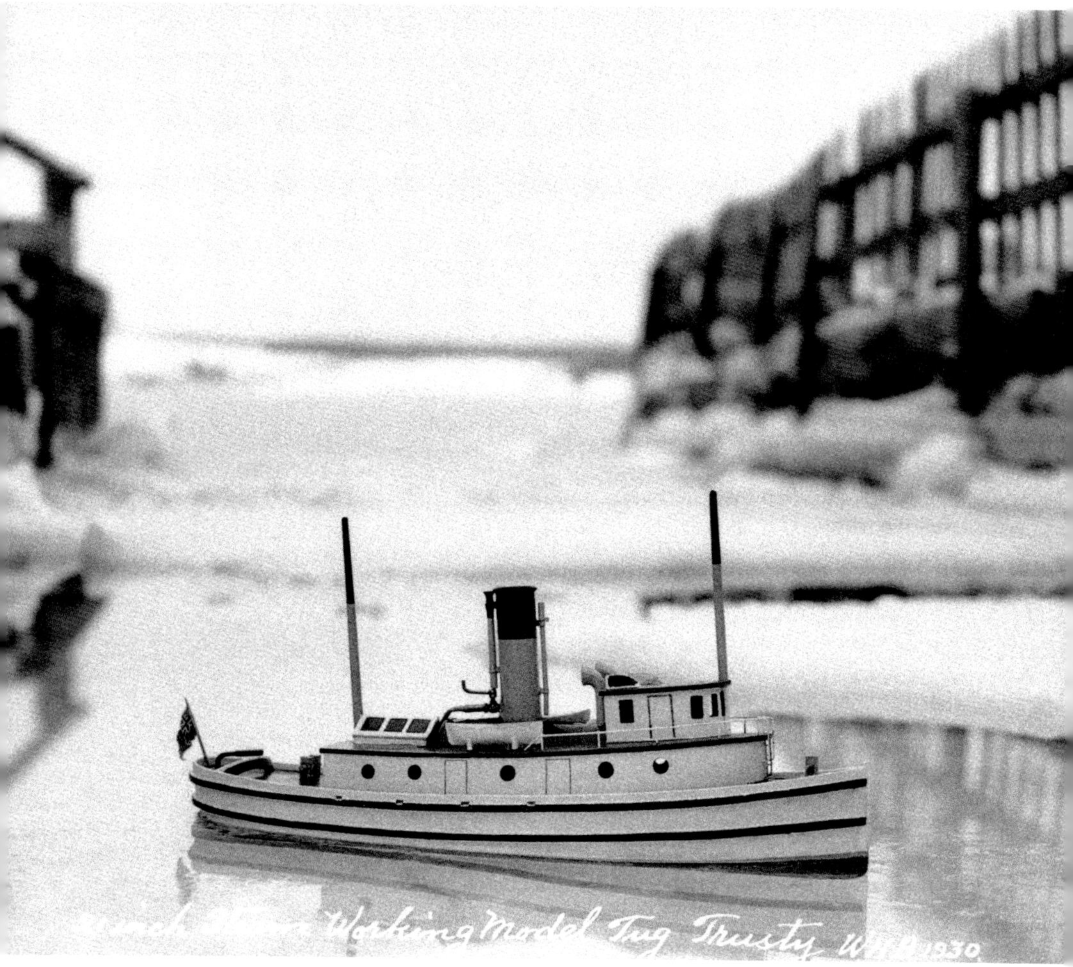
Working Model Tug Trusty
1930

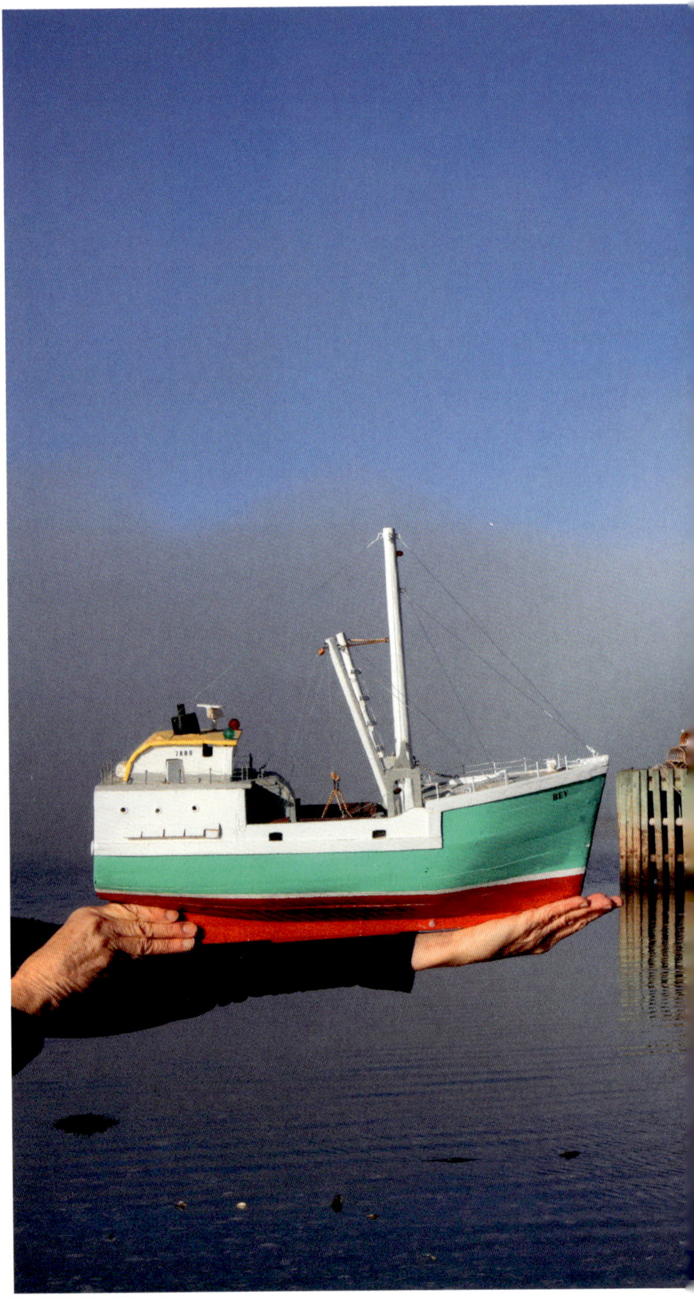

"BEV," SCALLOP DRAGGER

Roy Boutcher, Mahone Bay, Nova Scotia

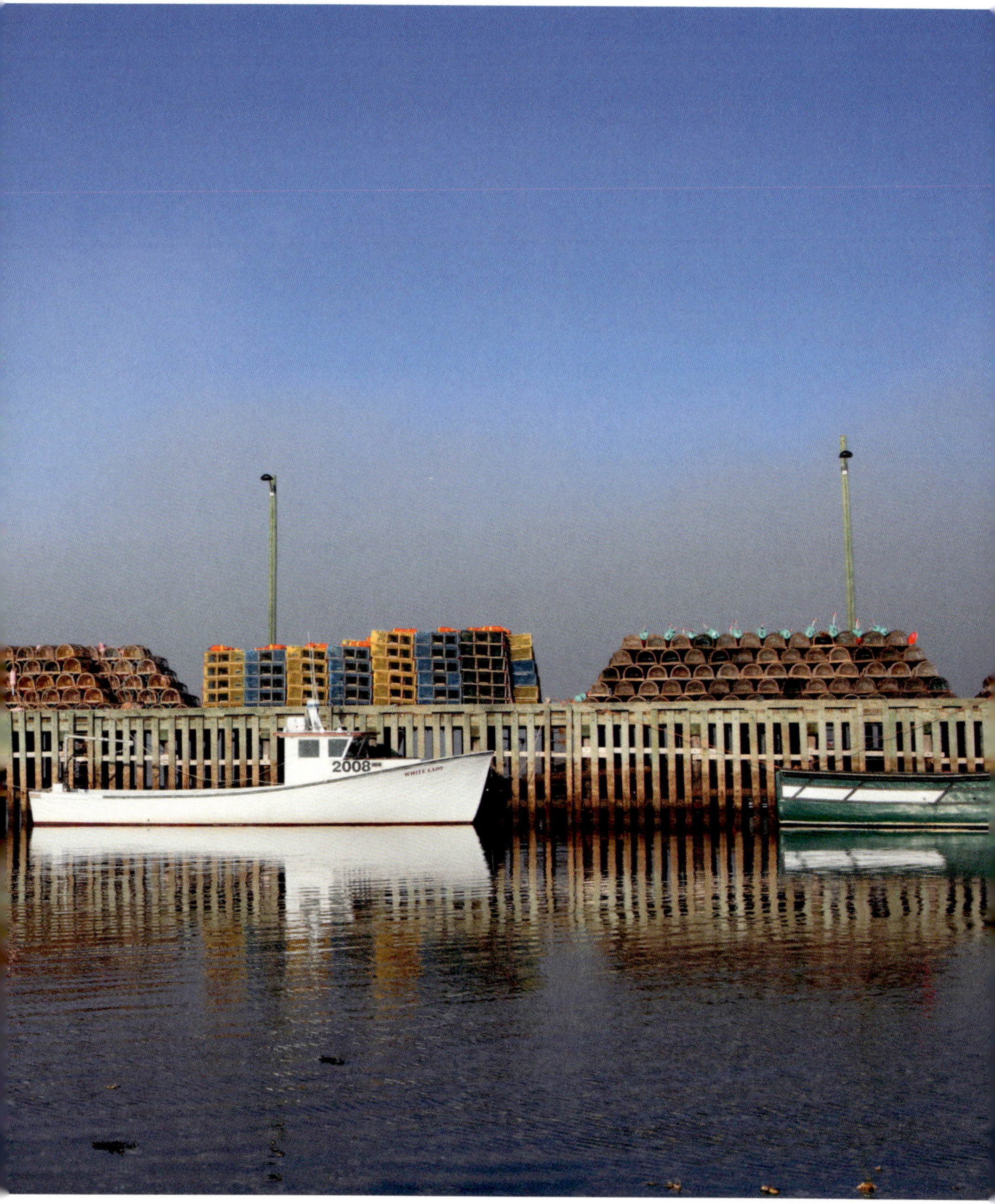
2008

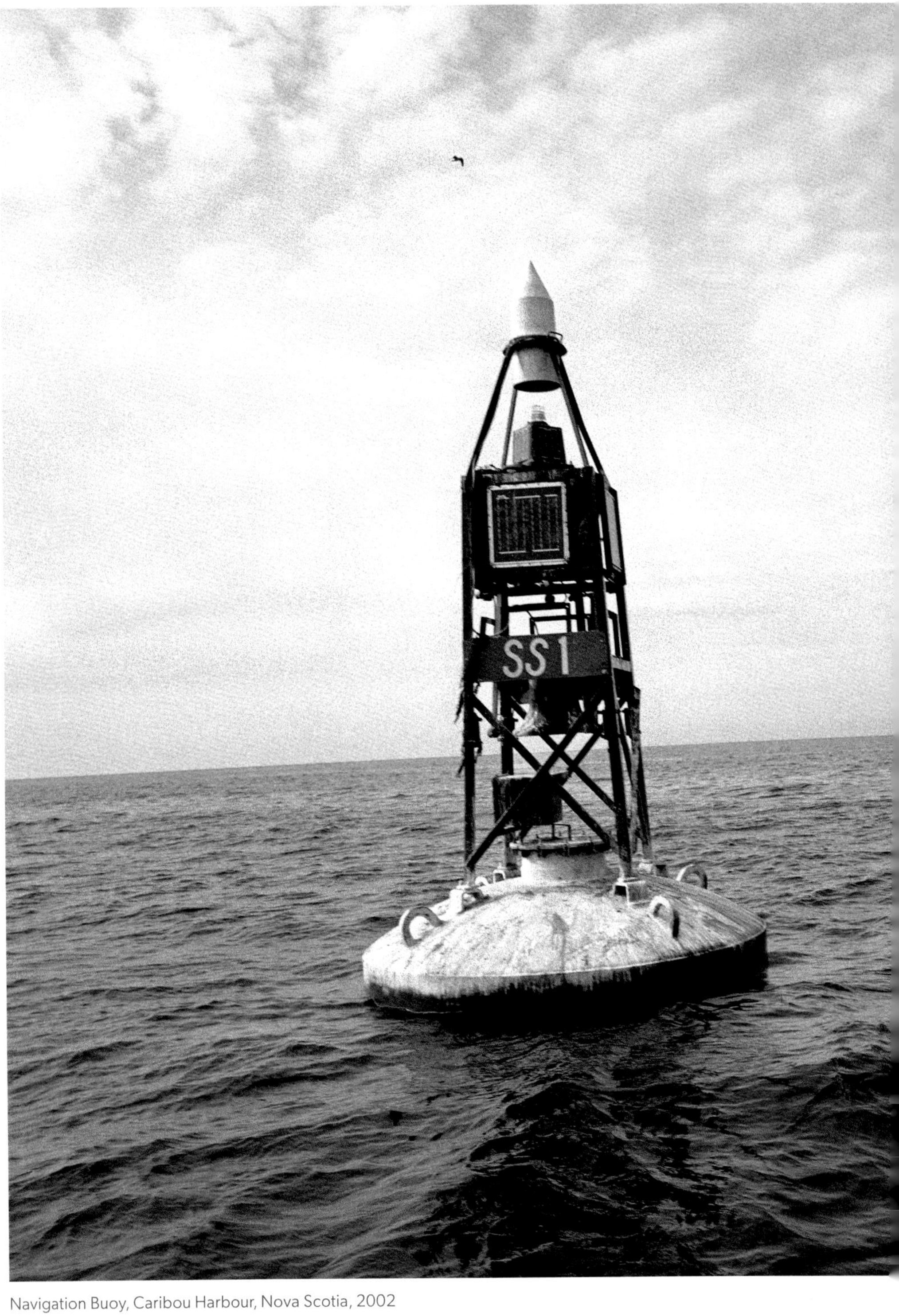

Navigation Buoy, Caribou Harbour, Nova Scotia, 2002

ACKNOWLEDGEMENTS

BOAT was created on beaches, harbours, and sites throughout Mi'kma'ki. I am thankful to live and work on this beautiful land, the traditional and unceded territory of the Mi'kmaq people.

Individuals and collections generously lent models to be photographed. *BOAT* would not be possible without the involvement of the Age of Sail Museum, Blacks Harbour Heritage Museum, the Fisheries Museum of the Atlantic, the Maritime Museum of the Atlantic, the Northumberland Fisheries Museum, and Ingenium (Canada's museums of science and innovation). Model makers Mark Boudreau, Greg Hiltz, Watson Kinckle, and Jim Turple shared their models and, along with Peggy Cameron, Robert Mellin, Eileen Newman, John Rae, and Robert Wilkie, welcomed my questions, contributing personal anecdotes, images, and histories that would be otherwise absent from our histories of these models.

Thank you, Adam Ehler, John Lyle, Lloyd and Randy Stewart, and Carson Welch for sharing models you crafted. Thank you, Captain Andrew J. Rae Marine Educational Services, Maureen Gibbons, the Levitt Goodman family, Ryan Langille, Debbie MacDonald, James MacLellan, Brian Maloney, and Don Miller for access to models you treasure. The Maritime Ship Modelers' Guild gave early and lively input.

Dave LeDrew, owner of the Newfoundland Emporium, and David Hawkins laid the foundation for my personal collection of models, which are among those photographed. The Bursey family lent family photographs to further tell their father's story, and exceptional historical photographs and documents were provided by the Beaton Institute at Cape Breton University and the Nova Scotia Archives. Thank you, Robert Wilkie, for access to your discharge books and seagoing experiences.

William Knight, agriculture and fisheries curator at Ingenium in Ottawa; Sara Spike, cultural historian; Peggy Gale, author, curator, critic; and Sue Goyette, poet and educator, applied their expertise and imaginations to tease meaning from model boats and my photographs.

Robert Mellin's insightful book, *Tilting: House Launching, Slide Hauling, Potato Trenching, and Other Tales from a Newfoundland Fishing Village,* began my journey with maritime material culture.

BOAT includes black-and-white photographs created early in my career. I am thankful to connect these experiences and art works across time. Friends and family were patient listeners and assistants. My partner David Craig floated models, catching light as needed. Our film production company, Site Media Inc., co-founded with David, expanded my access to maritime experiences. Filmmaker Marcia Connolly collaborated on our films *Pretend Not to See Me: the Art of Colette Urban* and *Strange and Familiar: Architecture on Fogo Island,* both shot in Newfoundland and key to the conception of *BOAT*.

Thank you, Charlie Arcon, Arscott family, Catherine Beaudette, Leonard and Shelley Bigney, Julia Bray, Doug Cowie, Max Dean, Eamonn Doorly, Larry Glenwright, Fred Hann, Wanda Koop, Dan Lander, Greg MacDonald, Roger Marsters, Jim McGrath, Donald Miller, Adrian Morrison, Marie Perrault, Richard Rhodes, Bill Stright, Ella Tetrault, Ben Verburgh, Rita Wilson, and Beulah Wright for insight and assistance; Dr. Daniel Walker for welcoming me into the Department of Ocean and Naval Architectural Engineering, Memorial University, to photograph; Sharon Babaian and the artifact handlers at Ingenium for facilitating access to the wind-tunnel models; Katarina Marinic and Paul Jerinkitsch for image preparation; James Harbeck for precise copy editing; Dian Day and William Knight for writing and editorial guidance throughout *BOAT*; and Lucas Elke and Type A Printing for your care and commitment to fine art.

Carter Pryor, thank you for your thoughtful design and willing collaboration from start to finish.

Thank you, publishers Robyn Lew and Jim Shedden of WORK BOOK and Goose Lane Editions, for believing in *BOAT*; and to York University for their support.

BOAT is supported in part by funding from the Social Sciences and Humanities Research Council.

Social Sciences and Humanities Research Council of Canada
Conseil de recherches en sciences humaines du Canada

Canada

BIO

Katherine Knight is an artist and filmmaker recognized for her landscape-based photographic works and documentary films about Canadian artists. Knight's award-winning films, produced by Site Media Inc., co-founded by David Craig and Katherine Knight, have screened worldwide through festivals, television broadcast, and media collections. In 2000, Knight received the Duke and Duchess of York Prize for excellence in photography from the Canada Council for the Arts. Knight's photographic works are in private and public collections including the National Gallery of Canada, Art Gallery of Nova Scotia, Museum London, Global Affairs Canada, Ottawa Art Gallery, Banff Centre for the Arts, Surrey Art Gallery, and the Canada Council Art Bank. Knight is a Professor Emeritus and Senior Scholar at York University and, after two decades of summer residence, lives full-time in Pictou County, Nova Scotia.

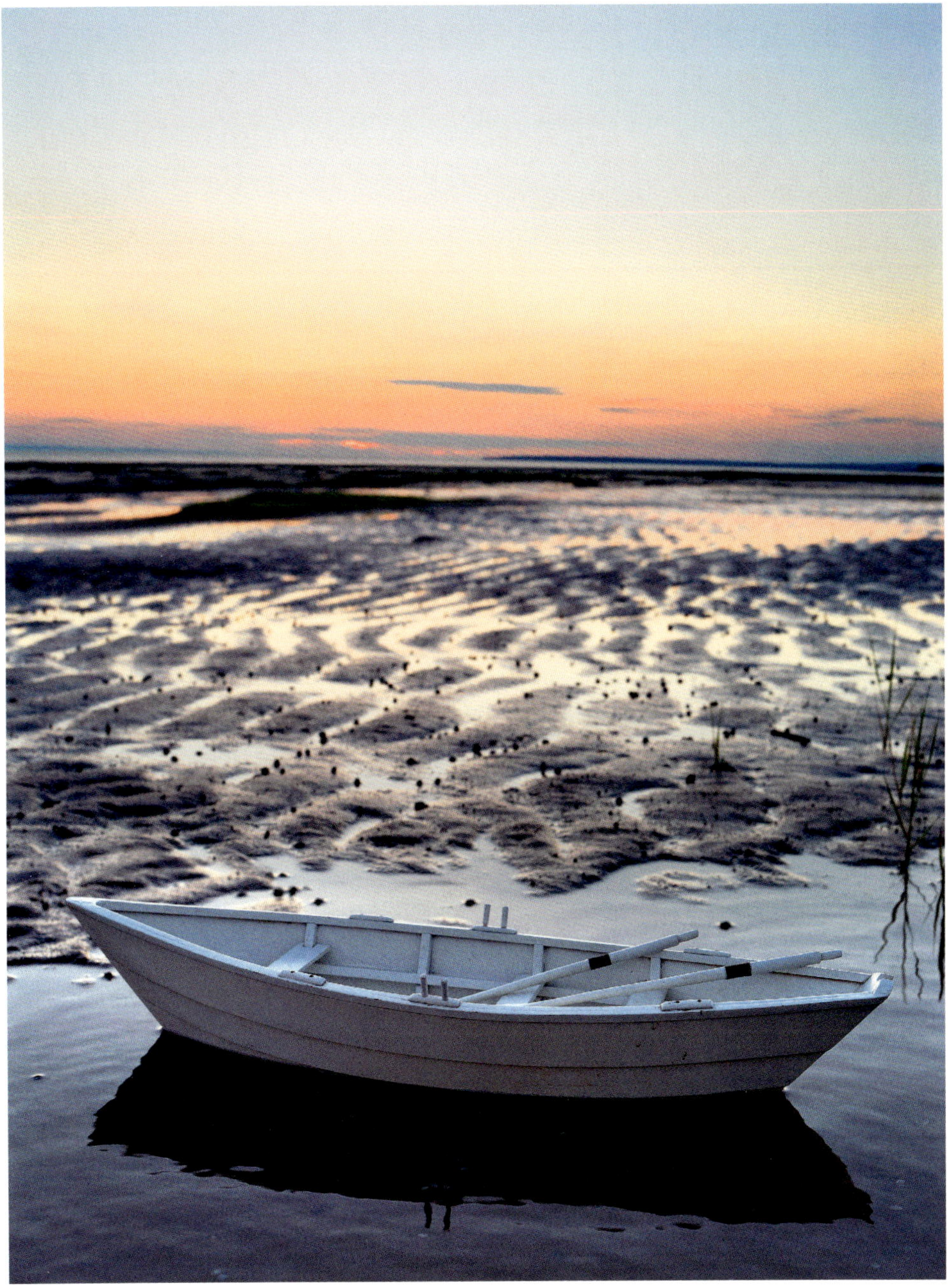

DORY

Maker unknown, Nova Scotia

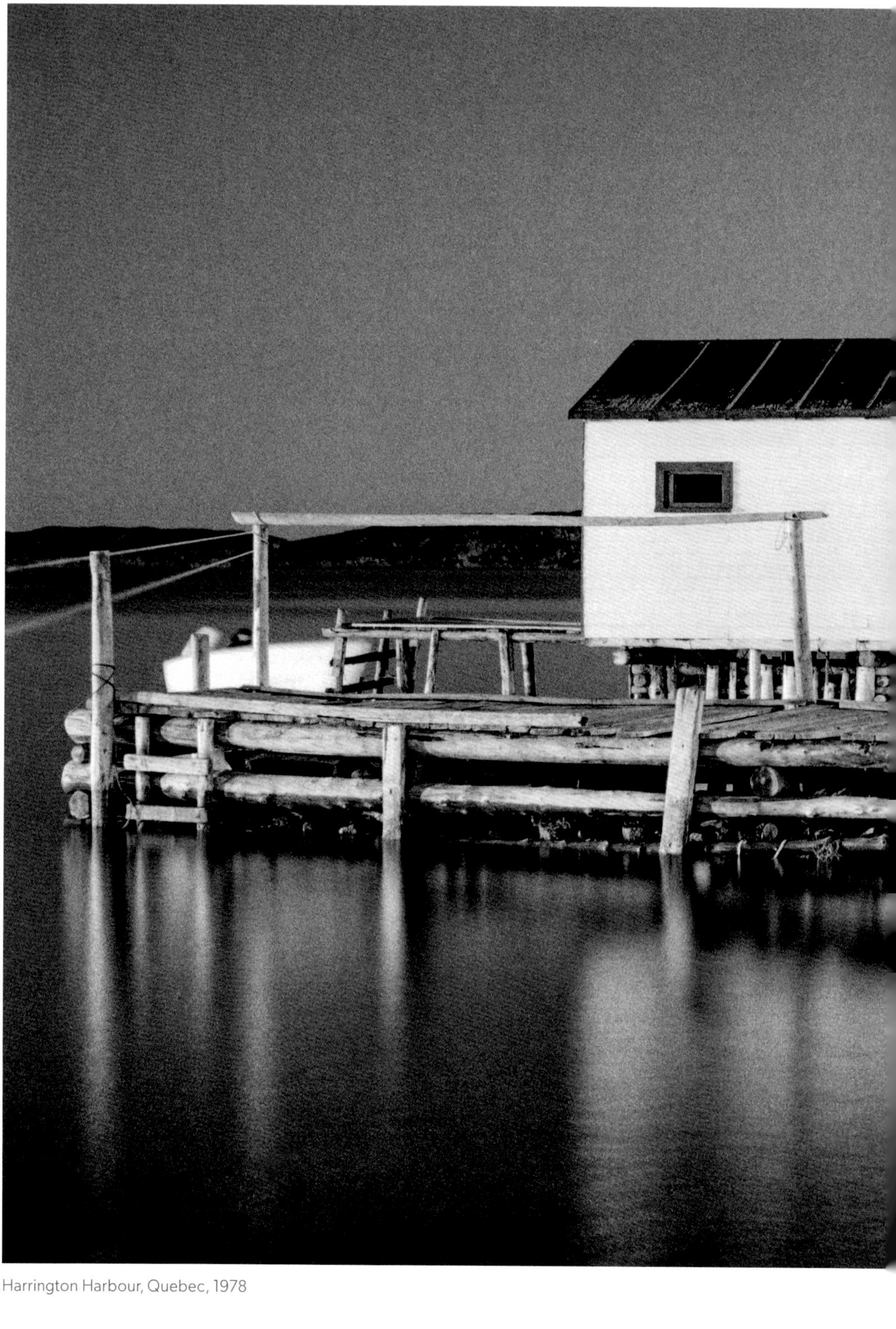

Harrington Harbour, Quebec, 1978

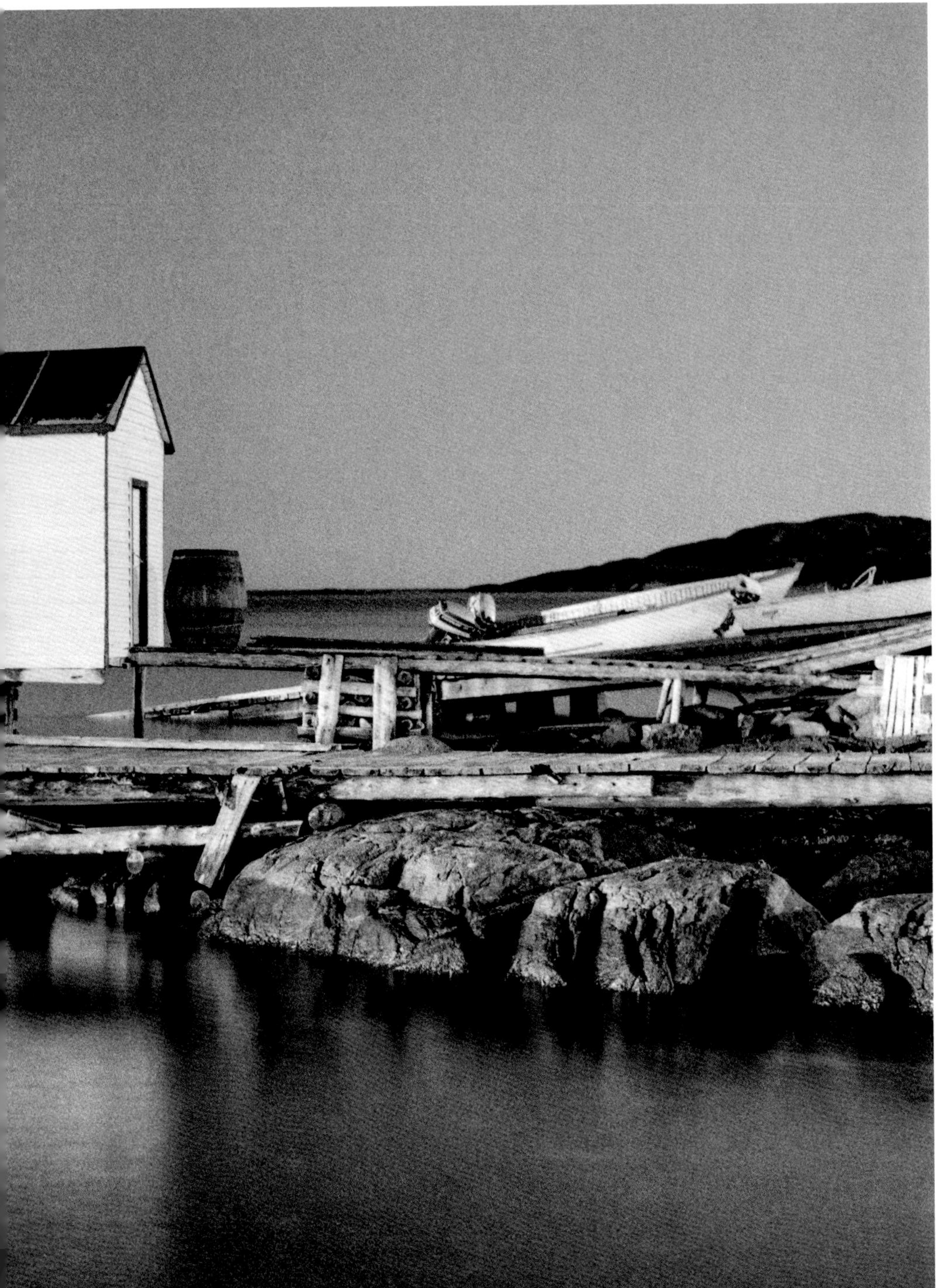

Published in 2025 by WORK BOOK and Goose Lane Editions.

WORK BOOK is a publishing collective led by Robyn Lew and Jim Shedden.

workbookeditions.com

Goose Lane Editions
500 Beaverbrook Court, Suite 330
Fredericton, New Brunswick
CANADA E3B 5X4
gooselane.com

Goose Lane Editions acknowledges the generous support of the Government of Canada, the Canada Council of the Arts, and the Government of New Brunswick.

Goose Lane is located on the unceded territory of the Wəlastəkwiyik whose ancestors along the with the Mi'kmaq and Peskotomuhkati Nations signed Peace and Friendship Treaties with the British Crown in the 1700s.

Printed and bound in Belgium.

10 9 8 7 6 5 4 3 2 1

ISBN: 978-1-77310-480-5

Library and Archives Canada Cataloguing in Publication

TITLE: BOAT / photographs by Katherine Knight.
NAMES: Knight, Katherine, 1955- author, photographer
IDENTIFIERS: Canadiana 20250179717 | ISBN 9781773104805 (hardcover)
SUBJECTS: LCSH: Ship models—Pictorial works. | LCSH: Photography of ship models. | LCSH: Photography, Artistic—21st century. | LCGFT: Photobooks.
CLASSIFICATION: LCC TR655.K65 2025 | DDC 779.092—dc23

Publication credits

EDITORS: Dian Day and Katherine Knight
BOOK DESIGNER: Carter Pryor
MANAGING EDITORS: Robyn Lew and Jim Shedden
COPY EDITOR: James Harbeck
PROOFREADER: Paula Sarson
PRE-PRESS: Paul Jerinkitsch
PRODUCTION EDITOR: Alan Sheppard, Goose Lane Editions
PRINTING & BINDING: Type A Print Inc.
PAPER STOCK: 170gsm Magno Matte
TYPEFACE: Gibson

FRONT COVER: DORY. Maker unknown, Nova Scotia
BACK COVER: DORY. Maker unknown, Nova Scotia
PAGE 1: PASSENGER BOAT. Maker unknown, Newfoundland and Labrador
INTERIOR COVER: Caribou Harbour, Nova Scotia
BELOW: COASTAL BOAT. Maker unknown, Nova Scotia

Additional photography credits

BEATON INSTITUTE: 62
BOUDREAU FAMILY: 136
BURSEY FAMILY: 120
NORTHUMBERLAND FISHERIES MUSEUM: 94
NOVA SCOTIA ARCHIVES: 72, 88, 144
ROBERT WILKIE: 44

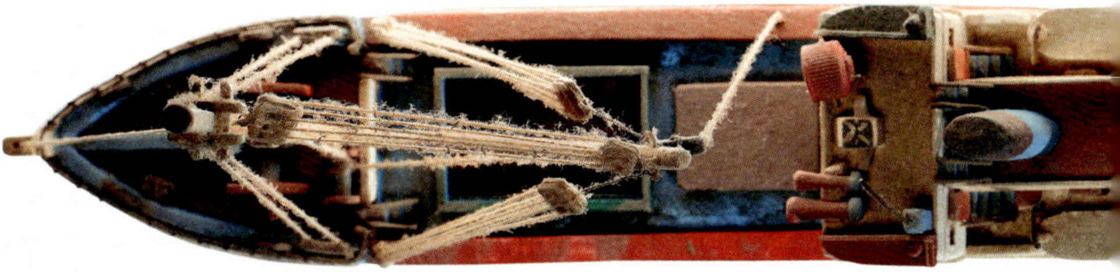